WILLIAM SHAKESPEARE
SELECTED
COMEDIES

INCLUDING:

ALL'S WELL THAT ENDS WELL

THE TAMING OF THE SHREW

THE WINTER'S TALE

THE COMEDY OF ERRORS

TWO GENTLEMEN OF VERONA

THE MERRY WIVES OF WINDSOR

LOVE'S LABOUR'S LOST

MARGARET RANALD

DEPARTMENT OF ENGLISH
QUEENS COLLEGE

MONARCH PRESS

A DIVISION OF SIMON & SCHUSTER, INC.
1 WEST 39th STREET
NEW YORK, NEW YORK 10018

Standard Book Number: 671-00629-0

Library of Congress Catalog Card Number: 65-7218

CONTENTS

INTRODUCTION

BIOGRAPHY OF SHAKESPEARE: The earliest documented fact about William Shakespeare is to be found in the town register for births, deaths, and marriages—the Parish Register of the church of Stratford-on-Avon—which lists the date of Shakespeare's christening as April 26, 1564. This, of course, is not the date of his birth, but scholars have generally considered Shakespeare's birthday to have been three days earlier, because it was customary to have children christened at the age of three days. In addition, there is a tradition that Shakespeare died on his birthday anniversary; the date of his death appears on his monument as April 23, 1616. The dramatist was the third child of a family which was well known in the neighborhood. His father, John Shakespeare, was a merchant and his mother came from a well-established land-owning family in Warwickshire, where Stratford is situated. For a time, the family prospered and John Shakespeare rose to a high position in the administration of the town. Unfortunately, his financial situation declined; consequently, in 1587, he was removed from his position on the city council and he seems to have had financial troubles until his death in 1601.

In the meantime, William Shakespeare was growing up in Stratford, then a town of about two thousand inhabitants—more important economically then than now. Traveling dramatic companies apparently stopped there, and it is possible that Shakespeare saw some of them. It was an important market town and boasted a good grammar school which Shakespeare probably attended. No school records concerning him survive, but, like most Elizabethan schoolboys he must have learned Latin, and probably some Greek. By the time he left school, he would have had to be fairly proficient in Latin. He did not go up to a university, possibly because of the financial reverses of his father.

The next important document concerning Shakespeare is a special marriage license issued on November 27, 1582, for the marriage of William Shakespeare and Anne Hathaway, who was eight years older than he. There seems to have been some reason for the haste with which the ceremony obviously took place because the first child of the couple was born in May 1583. Twins, named Hamnet and Judith, were born in 1585.

At this point, we enter the realm of undocumented conjecture. No documents at all are to be found for the period between 1585 and 1592; consequently, this period is called "the lost years." Certainly Shakespeare had been in Stratford in 1584, and probably again in 1585, for the christening of the twins. John Aubrey, the seventeenth-century antiquarian and gossip, said that "Shakespeare had been, in his younger years, a schoolmaster in the country." But Aubrey is not a trustworthy source. Another theory sends Shakespeare to the wars against the Spanish in the Low Countries, while yet another sends him to London where his initial job was that of holding horses for theatregoers. Probably the most frequently heard legend about Shakespeare concerns his hurried departure from Stratford after he allegedly had stolen some deer from the park of Sir Thomas Lucy of Charlecote. All these theories are no more than legend and should be treated with caution. In 1592, Shakespeare reappears in documents in a pamphlet written on his deathbed by the university wit, playwright, and journalist, Robert Greene. Greene attacked Shakespeare for his presumption in competing with his betters in playwriting. Undoubtedly, Shakespeare was by this time a threat to the university men who also were trying to make their living with their pens.

For the rest of his working life, Shakespeare wrote for, and acted with, a single dramatic company, The Lord Chamberlain's Company, which became known as the "King's Men" after the accession of King James I. All of Shakespeare's thirty-seven plays were written for this group which performed them in the public theatres, in private theatres, in private houses, and at court. Shakespeare provided them with one or two plays a year until 1612-13 and he was also a sharer in the profits of the company.

Exactly how much of his time Shakespeare spent in London and how much in Stratford is not known. He was probably in Stratford for the funeral of his son Hamnet in 1596, and possibly for that of his father in 1601. Certainly his financial affairs seem to have been well managed. He invested substantially in Stratford real estate; in 1597, he bought New Place, one of the largest and finest houses in the town. He probably returned to Stratford permanently about 1610, but his work was not finished as two more complete plays and parts of two others were written afterwards.

The actual circumstances of Shakespeare's death are not known; however, his monument gives the date of his death as April 23, 1616. A seventeenth-century tradition is that Shakespeare died of a fever contracted of a rather too merry meeting with the dramatist Ben Jonson and the poet Michael Drayton. Shakespeare's will, prepared some time before, left bequests to his two daughters, his friends and partners in the King's Men, and, of course, his wife. The oft-discussed bequest to Anne of the "second-best bed" has been taken to mean that the poet's marriage was unhappy, but such bequests were common, and, further, the bed was probably the one in which they themselves slept.

THE ANTI-STRATFORDIANS: Possibly because of the rather fragmentary evidence concerning the life of Shakespeare, an anti-Shakespeare, or anti-Stratfordian, school of thought has developed. In general, followers of this school protest that Shakespeare was too uneducated to have written the plays himself, and a subtle snobbery seems to dictate that any candidate put forward as the "real" Shakespeare must be of superior birth and education to the playwright. Some of the suggested authors include Christopher Marlowe, Francis Bacon, the Earl of Southampton, the Earl of Oxford, and Sir Walter Raleigh. The Baconian and the Oxford theories are two most popular, but most scholars prefer to accept Will Shakespeare, Gent., as the creator of the plays which bear his name.

THE TEXT OF SHAKESPEARE'S PLAYS: Some of Shakespeare's plays were printed during his lifetime. The texts published were of two kinds: (1) plays sold to printers by the King's Men, usually when it needed money because the theatres were closed due to the plague; (2) pirated plays, or stolen and unauthorized texts, which were often inaccurate, and sometimes issued by unscrupulous printers who wanted to cash in on the popularity of a play. Both kinds of texts were usually printed in modest-sized volumes and called "quartos," a word designating the size of the pages. The first kind of authorized text is usually called a "good quarto" and the pirated text a "bad quarto." Sometimes, a bad quarto was followed by a good quarto publication. Shakespeare's complete works were published in a large folio volume in 1623 by two of Shakespeare's friends, John Heminges and Henry Condell. Most of the comedies discussed in this book appeared in print for the first time in 1623.

THE PUBLIC THEATRE OF SHAKESPEARE'S DAY: Shakespeare's theatre was quite different from our own. It was an octagonal, or round, structure with three tiers of roofed galleries around the major section. The central portion was an unroofed yard, the "pit," in which spectators stood. These "standing room only" places cost the least (one penny—later, twopence), and the people who stood were often scornfully referred to as "groundlings"; they were believed by the more educated people to like nothing but clowning. This belief is not entirely supported by evidence. The roofed galleries, which contained seats, cost more the higher up the seat; by 1596, young gallants were sitting on the stage itself. Both men and women went to the theatre, but boys played all the women's roles in the plays. The stage projected almost thirty feet into the yard and was narrower at the front than at the back. The back half of the stage was roofed with thatch; the other half was left open. There was no proscenium arch and no front curtain, but there were curtains at the back between two sets of swinging doors which were placed at an angle to the stage. The curtain at the stage level formed the "inner stage" or "study" in which furniture properties were sometimes used, such as the bed in *Othello*. Above the "study," a projecting balcony was built with a curtain about four feet behind it forming another inner stage. The balcony, or "tarras," was useful for action such as that in the famous balcony scene in *Romeo and Juliet*. Open windows were set on the upper level over the doors, and they, too, could be used. Above the tarras, there was a smaller balcony with a railing and a curtain which was generally used as a musicians' gallery or for the upper deck of a ship. A collection of three gabled structures, the "huts," was on the very top of this structure creating a fourth level from which sound effects could be produced, and from which objects, such as thrones, could be lowered onto the stage. Above the huts a flagstaff held the flag of the theatre which was flown during performances. Behind the stage, the "tiring house" or dressing room for the actors was constructed, while underneath the stage was the "hell" which had machinery for raising and lowering the stage trap doors. In all, there were seven separate playing levels on the flexible Elizabethan stage.

Performances, announced with trumpet calls, in the afternoon started about two o'clock and generally lasted approximately two hours. Daylight was the only illumination in the public theatres, though candlelight was used for indoor performances at court and in the private theatres. The capacity of the theatre varied with the individual building, but it is probable that the Globe, Shakespeare's theatre, held between two and three thousand people. The building, however, was rarely filled to capacity except for a new play.

There were many advantages in this kind of theatre, and, in some ways, the physical characteristics of the building and the stage helped to dictate the form of the plays. Since there was no scenery, the stage represented any place the playwright chose. As a result, the action moved quickly from place to place and from scene to scene so that alternation of plot and subplot was much simpler than it is today. Also, the action could take place on several different playing levels. Elizabethan plays were, therefore, swift moving and were enhanced with poetry and ever-changing action rather than being hampered by scenery. Since there was no attempt at literal staging, sight and sound effects were evocative rather than endeavors to imitate realism. Further, the playwright himself, with language alone, was able to establish the sets in the imagination of the audience through he could not employ physical sets.

SHAKESPEARE'S WORK: In general, Shakespeare's work falls into four major periods, all of which are represented in this book. The first period, 1590-1594 includes history plays and the early farces, *The Comedy of Errors* and *The Taming of the Shrew*, as well as the early romantic comedies, *The Two Gentlemen of Verona* and *Love's Labour Lost*. The second period, 1595-1600, includes additional history plays, the great comedies, and *The Merry Wives of Windsor*, now definitely dated 1597. The third period, 1600-1608, is the period of Shakespeare's great tragedies, and his three unusual "problem plays," of which *All's Well That Ends Well* is an example. Even in comedy, Shakespeare seems to be concerned with the darker aspects of the human spirit, and it is only because *All's Well* and its companion piece, *Measure for Measure*, end happily that they are classified as "comedies." There is a great deal of bitterness and near tragedy in both. The final period, 1609-1613, seems totally different in tone from the former works. This is the time when Shakespeare is writing his dramatic romances, represented here by *The Winter's Tale*. The playwright is moving away from his earlier methods and is creating a new, symbolic, and reconciliatory kind of drama which is extremely subtle in its presentation of ideas. These late romances always contain elements of tragedy, but they conclude in reconciliation and, in their almost circular organization, they seem to represent the repetition and varied occurrences of life itself.

THE COMEDY OF ERRORS

THE PLAY: *The Comedy of Errors* is one of the few plays of Shakespeare which deals almost entirely with middle-class characters. It is also one of Shakespeare's earliest pieces, although we may not have it in its original form, and it is usually dated 1592-93. The play does not concern itself much with the study of character, except, in small measure, with that of Adriana, who does develop in the course of the play. On the whole, the play is a farce dependent upon action which becomes faster and more confusing until the tangle is unraveled in the last scene. If one grants the initial assumption that one pair of twins can be mistaken by everyone in the play, then it is a small concession to grant the second assumption, that these twins should have equally identical servants, and all the incidents follow from there with perfect, though absurd, logic. The comedy depends almost entirely on a superb sense of stagecraft and it is interesting to note the number of variations that Shakespeare manages to work on the theme of mistaken identity. Like most of Shakespeare's comedies, *Comedy of Errors* begins in sorrow and ends in joy with a grand finale in which all the characters are paired off. At the same time, however, Shakespeare manages to introduce a deeper note into the farcical play because of the near tragedy of Aegeon.

THE SOURCES: The main plot of the twins who cannot be told apart comes from *The Menaechmi* by the Roman playwright Plautus. Shakespeare, however, has brought in a subplot and added to the confusion by giving the twins equally indistinguishable servants. He has also used another play, the *Amphitruo* by Plautus, as a source for the situation of a husband locked out of his own house while his wife entertains another man. The frame narrative of the Aegeon–Aemilia plot comes from a third possible source, *Appolonius of Tyre*. Shakespeare lessened the part of the Courtezan in his play and gave Adriana, the wife of Antipholus of Ephesus, a sister, Luciana, possibly to add further doubling and, also, to give a romantic interest to the character of Antipholus of Syracuse. The character of Adriana, the shrew, is also contrasted with that of Aemilia, the abbess, who delivers a speech on wifely behavior.

THE TEXT: The play was first printed in the First Folio of 1623 and is Shakespeare's shortest play, having a mere 1,777 lines. The date of its composition is disputed; one critic believes that it was originally written about 1590 and later revised. The text itself is considered good, but the unevenness of poetic style lends some support to the revision theory, though J. Dover Wilson believes that the play in an abridgement of a much longer work. Possibly it was never meant for an entire evening's entertainment, but was instead an introductory piece, meant to precede another musical or dramatic performance.

THE PLOT: Aegeon, a merchant from Syracuse, has been arrested in Ephesus and condemned to death because he cannot pay the fine that is levied on all residents of his town if they are found in Ephesus. The Duke asks how he happened to come to Ephesus, knowing as he must of the enmity between the two towns. Aegeon then tells the Duke that he has come seeking his son. Some twenty-three years before, Aegeon's wife, Aemilia, gave birth in Epidamnum to identical twin sons. At the same time, a poor woman also gave birth to identical twin sons at the same inn, and Aegeon bought these twins to be servants to his own two sons. When his business in Epidamnum was completed, he and his wife set sail for Syracuse, but their ship was wrecked on the way home and they were separated. Aegeon saw Aemilia, with one of her own children and one of the poor boys, picked up by a different ship from a port other than the one to which he was taken. Uable to find the rest of the party, Aegeon reared the remaining twin and his servant, giving them the names of their respective brothers. But when they were eighteen years old, his son wished to search for his brother so he left home accompanied by his servant. That had been five years before. Aegeon has received no word, so he has set out to look for his son. The Duke is so touched that he gives the desolate Aegeon one extra day to raise the money for his fine.

In the meantime, Antipholus of Syracuse, with his servant Dromio, has arrived in Ephesus, and, in order to avoid the fate of travelers from Syracuse, has said that he is from Epidamnum. He sends Dromio of Syracuse away on an errand; then Dromio of Ephesus arrives and tells Antipholus of Syracuse to come home to dinner. Antipholus of Syracuse is angered and beats Dromio of Ephesus, thinking that he is chastising his own servant.

We are now introduced to two new characters, Adriana, the wife of Antipholus of Ephesus, and her sister Luciana. Adriana is angered that her husband has not yet arrived for dinner and then Dromio of Ephesus arrives saying, because of the preceding puzzling interview, that his master must be mad.

In the next scene, Antipholus of Syracuse meets his own servant again and taxes him with the behavior of his brother from Ephesus. This time, Dromio of Syracuse is beaten, but, on the arrival of Adriana and Luciana, the two men eventually accompany the women home to dinner. Antipholus of Ephesus and his Dromio now appear and ask to be let into their own house; they discover that they are locked out while the servant, Dromio of Syracuse, claims that they are already dining inside.

Antipholus of Ephesus is angry with his wife, but Balthazar, a friend, counsels patience. Antipholus of Ephesus is so furious that he decides to dine with a courtezan of his acquaintance and to give her the gold chain which he had previously promised to his wife. Luciana now appears with Antipholus of Syracuse and asks him to be kind to her sister, Adriana, who loves him dearly. In reply, Antipholus of Syracuse answers that he is most interested in Luciana herself, much to that young lady's horror, because she believes that her own brother-in-law is making love to her. Dromio of Syracuse then appears and tells his master about a kitchen wench who expresses love for him. Angelo, a goldsmith, arrives at this point and insists on giving Antipholus of *Syracuse* the gold chain he is carrying with him. Antipholus tries to pay him, but Angelo says that the matter can wait. The Syracusan then sends his Dromio to fetch a ship so that they can leave Ephesus.

In the next act, Angelo is being pressed for payment of a debt to a merchant, and he promises to get the money from Antipholus of *Ephesus* to whom, he thinks, he gave the gold chain. At this moment, Antipholus of Ephesus appears with his Dromio whom he sends to fetch a rope with which to chastise Adriana. Much to Angelo's rage, Antipholus of Ephesus disclaims all knowledge of the chain; therefore, Angelo has him arrested. Suddenly, Dromio of Syracuse appears and starts talking about the ship he has obtained for his own master. Enraged now, Antipholus of Ephesus sends this Dromio to Adriana to get money as payment for the debt he is supposed to have contracted. Adriana and Luciana are discussing the strange behavior of Antipholus of Syracuse (for they are both mistaken about his identity) when Dromio of Syracuse arrives. Despite her shrewish comments on her husband a moment earlier, Adriana immediately sends the required money by Dromio of Syracuse. On the way back, Dromio of Syracuse meets his master and hands him the money he has received from Adriana. While Antipholus of Syracuse is recovering from this shock, the Courtezan arrives and demands the ring she had given him at dinner. When he reacts in a totally mystified manner, the Courtezan thinks he must be mad and goes to inform Adriana.

By this time, Antipholus of Ephesus is under arrest and when his own servant arrives with the rope's end he had been sent for, and not the money Antipholus thinks he should have brought, another beating takes place. The scene reaches its high point of confusion when Adriana, Luciana, and the Courtezan, accompanied by a doctor, arrive to take Antipholus away as a madman. After some discussion, Antipholus and Dromio of Ephesus are taken to their home under guard. Antipholus and Dromio of Syracuse arrive at this time and are mistaken for their "mad" brothers. The two decide to leave Ephesus as quickly as possible.

The final act begins with the merchant and Angelo discussing the fact that Antipholus of Ephesus has not yet paid his debt; then the Syracusan pair appear and Angelo asks for his money. In the course of the discussion, Antipholus's honesty is questioned and he draws his sword to satisfy his honor. Adriana, Luciana, and the Courtezan arrive and the Syracusans take refuge in a nearby convent. Aemilia, the Abbess, comes out to see what the altercation is about and Adriana tells her that she is looking for her husband, who has gone mad. The Abbess then delivers a sermon on wifely conduct for Adriana's benefit, saying that her shrewish behavior has driven her husband mad; she then refuses to give Antipholus up to Adriana.

In desperation, and pushed by Luciana, Adriana beseeches the Duke to order the return of her husband. Luckily for her, the Duke happened to be passing on his way to observe the execution of Aegeon. After Adriana has finished her tale, Antipholus and Dromio of Ephesus appear and Antipholus tells his side of the story. The Duke is understandably mystified, but Aegeon thinks he has found his Syracusan son. Of course, there is more mistaken identity until the two pairs of twins confront each other and the confusion is cleared up. Then the Abbess reveals herself as Aegeon's long-lost wife, Aemilia. Overhelmed by these revelations, the Duke pardons Aegeon. Rejoicing is universal, Antipholus of Syracuse hints at marriage to Luciana, another round of confusion of identity takes place, and everyone leaves the stage for a feast, at which they will discuss the events of the past twenty-three years.

DETAILED SUMMARY OF "THE COMEDY OF ERRORS"

ACT I: SCENE 1

The play opens in the hall of the palace of the Duke of Ephesus in Greece, some time in the past. Aegeon, a merchant of Syracuse, has been arrested and brought before the Duke because he, an inhabitant of the enemy city, has dared to land in Ephesus. So great is the hatred between these two cities that no trade is permitted between them, and any resident of one city found in the other is either executed or forced to pay a heavy fine. Aegeon does not have enough money for the fine and, therefore, is condemned to death.

The Duke, however, is curious to discover from Aegeon what had led him into the city of his enemies. Aegeon explains at length that he is searching for his lost sons. Twenty-three years before, he had become the father of identical twin sons, who were born in Epidamnum when he and his wife were there on business. At the smae time, another woman, of a lower class, gave birth at the same inn to identical twin sons, whom Aegeon bought from their exceedingly poor parents to be servants for his own children. On the way back to Syracuse, their ship was wrecked, and Aegeon and his wife, each with one of their own children and one servant child, were separated. Aegeon and his two babies were picked up by one ship, while his wife and the two children with her were rescued by a vessel from another city. Both boats sailed to their home ports and the two halves of the party had not seen each other again.

Aegeon had brought up the two children he had with him, one his own, and the other a servant child, both of whom he named for their lost brothers. But when Aegeon's son reached the age of eighteen, he and his attendant both decided that they would like to go in search of their respective brothers. They set out on their quest. They had been gone for five years, and Aegeon has been waiting to hear from them. He has finally set out in search of them. Despite the laws fining the inhabitants of Syracuse he has, therefore, come to Ephesus in the hope of finding the boys.

This story touches the Duke's heart and he allows Aegeon one more day of life so that he may be able to raise his fine. If he cannot, he must die. Aegeon leaves gloomily, because he cannot see any chance of buying his life; furthermore, he is so sorrowful that life no longer means much to him.

COMMENT: This scene reveals the events that took place in the past which have a bearing on the action of this play. It is, therefore, a piece of *dramatic exposition* (a manner of conveying facts in the most natural manner possible) achieved through the use of a court-room situation in which the accused gives evidence in his own defense and answers the questions put to him by the judge, in this case the Duke. The past is almost as important as the present in this play, so the events are detailed as carefully and as precisely as possible. The entire present situation is also established. The athmosphere of this first scene is one of sorrow rather than comedy, and, at first, the audience is not given any indication of the comic events ahead. The Duke's character is also revealed as merciful and sympathetic, but he must, nevertheless, enforce the laws. Aegeon is also introduced, but he disappears from the action until the final scene.

SUMMARY: The opening scene has the following purposes:

1. It serves as exposition, an introduction to the events of the play in which all the relevant occurrences of the past are revealed to the audience.

2. It establishes the Duke as a man of mercy who must also, as a ruler, be a man of justice in enforcing the law, no matter how deeply his own personal sympathies are engaged.

3. It indirectly introduces most of the principal characters who will be involved in the future confusions in the action.

4. It explains the current situation of the missing twin sons and twin servants in such a way that the audience can more or less understand what is happening as the plot becomes more complex.

ACT I: SCENE 2

This scene takes place in the Mart of Ephesus and the first characters to appear are the First Merchant, Antipholus of Syracuse, and his slave, Dromio of Syracuse. The Merchant warns Antipholus that his goods may be confiscated if his town of origin is discovered, and suggests that he claim Epidamnum as his native city (the town was where the twins were born). He also mentions, without giving his name, the forthcoming fate of Aegeon.

COMMENT: This opening speech by the Merchant introduces Antipholus of Syracuse and refers to the first scene to corroborate the statements made there. It also lets the audience know that there are now three Syracusans in Ephesus: Antipholus, Dromio, and Aegeon. No connection is specifically made between the young men and Aegeon at this point. Their relationship becomes clear as the play progresses.

Antipholus of Syracuse then orders his slave, Dromio of Syracuse, to take the money from the Merchant to the Centaur Inn. Dromio of Syracuse departs as he is ordered; at the exit of the Merchant, who arranges a meeting for a later time, Antipholus of Syracuse laments the loss of his brother.

> **COMMENT:** This expression of sorrow identifies Antipholus of Syracuse as the son of Aegeon seeking his lost twin. It also prepares for the entrance of the next character.

Dromio of Ephesus, the double of his brother from Syracuse, then enters and, mistaking Antipholus of Syracuse for his own master, he upbraids him for not having returned to his home and his wife in time for dinner. Antipholus of Syracuse, thinking he is talking to his own Dromio, asks about the money he had given his servant for safekeeping. Dromio of Ephesus is bewildered.

> **COMMENT:** This is the first scene in which mistaken identity is the most important element. There will be many others in the course of the play and Shakespeare manages to present almost every possible combination given two sets of identical twins in a play. Note that Shakespeare keeps his audience momentarily ignorant of the identity of the two Dromios, that is, until this one opens his mouth.

Dromio of Ephesus again tells Antipholus of Syracuse that his wife is waiting at home for him. Antipholus laughs and asks about the money. After more instances of complete mutual incomprehension, complicated by the witty punning of the slave, Antipholus of Syracuse beats Dromio of Ephesus until he runs off.

> **COMMENT:** This beating of the servants was a common humorous device in *Plautine comedy* (comedy based largely on slapstick and mistaken identity written by the Roman playwright Plautus) on which this Shakespearean comedy is based. The beating is not to be considered seriously. Dromio of Ephesus is also shown to be a *stock character* (a conventional character type), such as the witty and clever slave of Plautus and Terence in the Roman drama. We also hear about the wife of Antipholus of Ephesus. Note how Shakespeare announces characters in advance of their entrances.

Antipholus of Syracuse then departs, fearing that his slave has either lost or stolen the money he had been given.

SUMMARY: This scene has many important functions in advancing the plot of the play:

1. It introduces the characters: Antipholus of Syracuse and Dromio of Syracuse.

2. It corroborates the situation in Act I, scene i, and helps establish Antipholus of Syracuse as Aegeon's son.

3. It introduces Dromio of Ephesus and also points forward to the possibility of further confusions, this time of the Antipholi.

4. It shows the *comic devices* which will be used frequently in the play: mistaken identity, dialogue at cross purposes, and puns.

5. It establishes the character of Dromio of Ephesus as typical of that of the witty slave of Roman comedy.

6. It reveals the existence of the "wife" for Antipholus.

7. It refers to major characters before they appear, thus linking this scene with the preceding and succeeding scenes.

ACT II: SCENE 1

This scene takes place in the house of Antipholus of Ephesus and begins with a debate between Adriana, the wife who was mentioned in the preceding scene, and her sister Luciana. In the course of conversation, the characters of the two women are revealed.

> COMMENT: Adriana is a rather suspicious, jealous, and, at times, almost a shrewish wife. As we watch her in the course of the play she develops a definite personality; although she is, in some ways, a stock character, she is the most fully developed personage in the play. The other characters exist for their actions, while Adriana is important also for what she says, what she is, and what she thinks.

Luciana and Adriana discuss the relative positions of men and women in society—particularly in marriage. Adriana asks why men should have more liberty than women, while Luciana speaks in favor of the subordinate position of women, drawing her examples from "The beasts, the fishes and the winged fowls. . . ."

> COMMENT: These two women are contrasted with each other and represent the two sides of the debate on the position of women. This debate was by no means a new one then, and it continues to the present day. According to Elizabethan books of behavior and courtesy (which aimed to teach not only manners, but also practical matters of morality and, on occasion, philosophy), the position of woman ought to be inferior to that of man, who was created as a superior being. Staunch supporters of the equality of women disagreed.

Dromio of Ephesus arives and tells in a witty and rather indirect manner of the treatment he has received from Antipholus of Syracuse. He is still convinced that he had been speaking to his own master, Antipholus of Ephesus. In her sadness, shame, and anger, Adriana launches into a speech berating her absent Antipholus, complaining that there is no reason for her to remain faithful to her husband since he is not faithful to her.

COMMENT: These speeches continue the complications of mistaken identity. The character of Adriana is further revealed by the way she manufactures many of her reproaches in her suspicious mind. We learn later that her accusations are in a way justified, but she, herself, is partly to blame for the result.

SUMMARY: The importance of this scene lies in the following developments:

1. The chaarcter of Adriana is revealed to us as being spoiled by "mad jealousy."

2. The remarks of Luciana lend a balance and a contrast to the comments of her sister. As a result, Shakespeare gives his audience both sides of a popular debate of the time.

3. The complications of the mistaken identity device are continued, even in the absence of most of the characters involved. Since the women accept the remarks of Dromio of Ephesus at their face value, the confusion is heightened.

ACT II: SCENE 2

The next scene takes place in a public place in Ephesus. Antipholus of Syracuse meets his own servant, Dromio of Syracuse, and he repeats most of the discussion with Dromio of Ephesus in Act I, scene ii. This time it is the other Dromio who is completely mystified, and another debate in which the chaarcters are at cross purposes begins. Dromio of Syracuse proves himself to be a worthy brother to his Ephesian counterpart, possessing the same kind of wit.

COMMENT: This section introduces other confusions. The first is between Antipholus of Syracuse and his own personal servant, Dromio of Syracuse, and it is accompanied by mutual misunderstanding. The second misunderstanding is a variation on the same theme because it involves two pairs of characters. The fact that both women are mistaken in the indentity of the Syracusans makes the likeness of the two sets of twins the more remarkable and the more credible. We learn later in the play that the Ephesian pair have never known of the existence of their Syracusan counterparts because they were taken away from their mother at birth. Consequently, the confusion of the Ephesians is better motivated than that of the Syracusans.

SUMMARY: This scene serves the following purposes:

1. It compounds the confusions of identity by showing the likeness between the two Dromios.

2. It defines the character of Dromio of Syracuse as that of another clever slave whose wit is based on punning.

3. It adds a further dimension to the complication by having both Adriana

and Luciana mistake the identity of the two Antipholi, an error which hints at their astonishing physical likeness.

4. The character of Adriana is developed further; while she seems suspicious, we can feel a little sympathy for her. She is by no means the usual figure of a shrew.

ACT III: SCENE 1

This scene takes place outside the house of Antipholus of Ephesus whom we meet for the first time.

> **COMMENT:** He has been talked about a lot, but Shakespeare has retained a little extra suspense and has allowed further complications by keeping him off stage as long as possible.

The opening speeches of Antipholus of Ephesus reveal his character and also show his awareness of the shrewishness of his wife, "when I keep not hours." In fact, Antipholus of Ephesus finds himself making up an alibi to explain his late arrival. A further complication is introduced now, because his servant, Dromio of Ephesus, is confused between the two Antipholi. Further characters appear in the persons of Balthazar, the Merchant, and Angelo, the goldsmith. Because Antipholus of Syracuse and his Dromio are currently at dinner in the house of Antipholus of Ephesus, the rightful husband and his Dromio are locked out of their own house. Antipholus of Ephesus shows himself to be a man of singularly short temper when he threatens to break down the door. He is restrained by Balthazar who mentions the "sober virtue, years and modesty" of Adriana. However, in his anger at being shut out, Antipholus of Ephesus proposes to Balthazar that they go to dinner with "a wench of excellent discourse, Pretty and witty; wild, and yet, too, gentle: . . ." It is this woman with whom Adriana has often suspected her husband of misconduct. Antipholus of Ephesus claims that the accusations are unjustified, but, in order to spite his wife, he will give the Courtezan a gold chain that he has ordered for Adriana.

> **COMMENT:** This scene introduces us to Antipholus of Ephesus and shows us his character and furious temper. It also comments on Adriana. Her husband implies that her constant suspicion and her accusations of misconduct with the "wench" have led him to want to dine with the girl. Note, however, that Balthazar seems to have a totally different view of Adriana, and sees her as a virtuous woman.

SUMMARY: This amusing scene is important for the advancement of the plot and it serves the following purposes:

1. It introduces Antipholus of Ephesus and his friends.

2. It introduces us to the "wench" at the Porpentine Inn before she actually appears.

3. It gives two different opinions of Adriana which show us that she is not merely the stock figure of the shrewish wife. Here, Shakespeare has taken pains to balance the comments in order to develop a character. It is unusual that such a multidimensional creation should appear in a farce which depends so heavily upon situation comedy.

4. It also shows the character of Antipholus of Ephesus as possessing a certain vengeful streak. We should not, however, make too much of this fact, because the situation with the Courtezan is largely revised for further dramatic complication.

ACT III: SCENE 2

This scene takes place before the house of Antipholus of Ephesus, as did the last one. On this ocasion, we have Luciana, the apostle of subservience in a woman, upbraiding Antipholus of Syracuse because he seems to have forgotten the office of a husband to his supposed "wife," Adriana. In reply, Antipholus of Syracuse expresses an interest in Luciana herself. The lady is appalled, because she sees the situation as one of a husband who is unfaithful to his wife, and one who woos her sister in the bargain.

> **COMMENT:** Shakespeare has managed to work another change in the matter of mistaken identity and dialogue at cross purposes. Here, he has compounded Adriana's accusations of her husband's infidelity by having Antipholus of Syracuse declare his interest in Luciana.

Dromio of Syracuse then enters and discusses in a crudely witty manner his meeting with Nell, the kitchen wench, whom, incidentally, we never meet.

> **COMMENT:** The unabashedly physical nature of Dromio of Syracuse's "geographical" exploration of Nell is built up as a contrast to the poetical and idealized passion that his master seems to feel for Luciana.

Angelo, the goldsmith, then appears and offers Antipholus of Syracuse a golden chain that Antipholus of Ephesus has ordered for his wife, Adriana. This is the same chain that the Ephesian Antipholus has decided to give to the Courtezan. The confused Antipholus of Syracuse accepts the chain, offering to pay for it, but, to his surprise, Angelo says he will wait for payment until Antipholus's "wife" has seen it. Warning Angelo that he should have taken the cash when it was offered, Antipholus of Syracuse notes that "a man here needs not live by shifts" (stratagems, tricks). He plans to escape from Ephesus as quickly as possible.

SUMMARY: This scene has several important purposes:

1. It develops interest in Antipholus of Syracuse and shows his interest in Luciana, the sister of Adriana. This passion is described in a highly poetic and idealistic manner. It also points up a further likeness between the two Antipholi in their being attracted to sisters.

2. It introduces a further complication and gives more evidence of the apparent matrimonial infidelity of Antipholus of Ephesus.

3. It underlines the amusing nature of the conventions of idealized love and expressions of it by employing the "affair" between Dromio of Syracuse and a fat, coarse, kitchen maid as contrast. The terms in which the situation is expressed act as a deliberate *counterpoint* (contrast in terms) to the affair of Antipholus of Syracuse.

4. It produces the gold chain which Antipholus of Ephesus had promised to Adriana. This chain will be important later as tangible evidence in disentangling the complications of the play.

ACT IV: SCENE 1

This scene takes place a short time later in a public place, or a place in the Mart, and it begins to emphasize the importance of the chain first produced in the preceding scene. Angelo, the goldsmith, is, himself, being pressed for payment of a debt to another merchant. Angelo promises the money by five in the evening, by which time he expects that Antipholus of Ephesus will have paid him for the chain.

> **COMMENT:** This part of the scene is a purely dramatic contrivance and it acts as a bridge for the audience, recalling past events and moving on to new action.

Antipholus of Ephesus and his Dromio enter. Antipholus is still angry at his wife's treatment of him, so he orders his Dromio to buy a rope's end with which to chastise his wife "and her confederates."

> **COMMENT:** Some of Adrianna's shrewish attitude is again shown to be justified. Considerable debate had taken place in England concerning the right of a husband to beat his wife. Legally, the practice was permitted, but, on the whole, writers on matrimony advised against it because such corporal punishment could cause enmity between husband and wife.

Angelo than asks Antipholus of Ephesus to pay for the chain and presents him with the bill. Initially, Antipholus of Ephesus suggests that Angelo take the chain to Adriana and have her give him the money, but upon being told that the chain is already in his possession and that, therefore, payment is due immediately, Antipholus becomes angry. Angelo calls for the police. At this point, Dromio of Syracuse, arrives, mistakes Antipholus of Ephesus for his own master, and reports that he has now procured and provisioned a ship for their departure. By this time, Antipholus of Ephesus, who has been mistaken for his brother by two different people in the course of a few minutes, is understandably bewildered. He tells Dromio of Syracuse that he had sent him for a rope's end, an order that the servant denies having received. The arrested Antipholus then sends Dromio of Syracuse to Adriana to obtain the money required for Angelo.

SUMMARY: This scene has important implications for the unwinding of the plot.

1. It emphasizes the importance of the gold chain.

2. It concentrates on Antipholus of Ephesus, his arrest, and his later confinement as a madman.

3. It repeats the confusion of Angelo between the two Antipholi.

4. It adds the confusion of Antipholus of Ephesus and the two Dromios.

5. It has Antipholus of Ephesus confuse the two Dromios.

ACT IV: SCENE 2

This scene takes place in the house of Antipholus of Ephesus almost simultaneously with the previous one. Luciana tells Adriana of the declaration of affection she had received from Antipholus of Syracuse when she had rebuked him for mistreating his "wife." Adriana is angered and threatens her husband with a tongue-lashing. When Dromio of Syracuse arrives and asks for money to pay Angelo and secure the release of Antipholus of Ephesus, Adriana's attitude changes completely. She immediately sends the money by Dromio, whom she, of course, thinks to be her husband's servant, and tells him to bring his master home immediately.

SUMMARY: This scene serves three purposes:

1. It compounds the confusion concerning Luciana, Adriana, and the two Antipholi.

2. It repeats the confusion concerning the two ladies and the two Dromios.

3. It permits the development of a further complexity in the character of Adriana, who immediately believes ill of her husband, but who, just as quickly, sends money for his release.

ACT IV: SCENE 3

This scene follows the previous one immediately and begins with the mystification of Antipholus of Syracuse when he finds himself so well known in Ephesus that he is even addressed by his name.

> **COMMENT:**   The fact that Antipholus of Syracuse does not think of the answer at this point may be considered a structural weakness in the play since he knew he had a twin brother. Shakespeare apparently wished to save all his answers for a grand final scene.

Dromio of Syracuse appears and is overjoyed to see his master out of the hands of the law, as he thinks. He then gives him the money that Antipholus of Ephesus had told him to obtain from Adriana. At this point, the nameless Courtezan from the Portentine, with whom Antipholus had dined, appears and asks for the return of the ring she had given her guest at dinner or for the chain that she had been promised. When Antipholus of Syracuse insults her, as does his servant, she remains on stage to make an angry speech which sums up the general confusions of the day insofar as the two Antipholi are concerned.

SUMMARY: This scene adds further confusions and contributes to the advancement of the plot.

1. Antipholus of Syracuse is mystified at finding himself well known in Ephesus.

2. Dromio of Syracuse mistakes his master for Antipholus of Ephesus who has been arrested.

3. The Courtezan mistakes Antipholus of Syracuse for his brother, who had dined with her earlier in the day.

4. Another tangible item is introduced: the Courtezan's ring, which she had given to Antipholus of Ephesus. Now each of the twins has a piece of jewelry which will later aid in their personal identification.

ACT IV: SCENE 4

This scene takes place in the public street along which Antipholus of Ephesus is being taken by the arresting officer. With the arrival of Dromio of Ephesus, further complications develop. He proudly returns with the rope's end, only to find that he should have brought money from Adriana to free his master. Suddenly, the complications for Antipholus of Ephesus reach a climax with the simultaneous arrival of Adriana, Luciana, the Courtezan, and Pinch, the doctor. The Courtezan claims that Antipholus is mad, and Adriana asks Dr. Pinch to conjure against the evil spirit which caused his madness.

> **COMMENT:** Since madness was often held to be the result of possession by a devil, one cure was to call up the evil spirit and to drive it from the body of the possessed person.

Antipholus's behavior lends color to the belief that he is mad when he cuffs the doctor and accuses him of having dined with Adriana while he himself had been locked out of the house. Adriana counters by saying that Antipholus of Ephesus dined at home, but in turn Antipholus is supported in his story by Dromio of Ephesus. Antipholus then accuses Adriana of having arranged with the goldsmith to have him arrested, a charge which Adriana denies, calling Luciana to witness that she had given the money requested to Dromio who, of course says that he was merely sent to fetch a rope's end. Antipholus of Ephesus threatens violence, insults Adriana, and finally Pinch and his henchmen want to bind him. The officer, however, refuses to relinquish his prisoner in case he might himself become liable for the debt to the goldsmith. But Adriana, whose tongue is momentarily softened, offers to pay whatever debt her mad husband might have contracted. The identity of the creditor, Angelo, is established, and the Courtezan again explains the matter of the ring and the chain.

> **COMMENT:** This scene carries the complication for Antipholus of Ephesus to its highest point. At the same time, it serves as exposition to recall to the audience the precise nature of the events.

Antipholus and Dromio of Syracuse then appear and are mistaken for their brothers. The women and the officer flee from what they consider to be a pair of madmen. Dromio of Syracuse, the sharp practitioner, wants to remain in Ephesus because he likes the rich gifts that seem to be forthcoming there, but Antipholus of Syracuse is more wary and decides to leave.

SUMMARY: This scene raises the complications to the highest point of complete confusion. The next act can only unwind the plot.

1. It has Antipholus of Ephesus confuse the two Dromios once more.

2. It culminates in the accusation that Antipholus of Ephesus is mad, and, certainly, his behavior would seem to affirm this belief. He is then removed in bonds.

3. It shows that Adriana is not really the shrew she pretends to be. She accepts the possibility that her husband's insults may be the result of his madness, and she offers to pay his debt.

4. It summarizes the most recent confusions and restates the matters of the ring and of the chain. The audience may now expect these trinkets to be of considerable importance.

5. It concludes with another confusion between the sets of Syracusan brothers and the Ephesian ones.

ACT V: SCENE 1

This scene takes place about five in the afternoon on the same day outside the Priory. It begins with Angelo's apologies to the Merchant; he explains that he has not yet received payment for the chain he made. At this point, Antipholus of Syracuse enters wearing the chain, and Angelo asks in an injured tone why the young man had disclaimed knowledge of it. The mystified Antipholus of Syracuse denies the charge, which is repeated by the Merchant, and threatens to fight to defend his honor. The Syracusans then rush into the nearby Priory for sanctuary.

> **COMMENT:** Antipholus of Syracuse, a gentleman, has been "given the lie" in dueling terms, which means that his honesty has been questioned. As a result, he must fight a duel in order to avenge the insult. *Sanctuary* meant that evildoers or people pursued by their

enemies who sought refuge in a church, a convent, or a monastery, would be immune to the clutches and penalties of the law as long as they remained inside.

Adriana and Luciana then appear and mistake the Syracusans for the Ephesian pair. They enlist the assistance of the Abbess and tell her of the "madness" of Antipholus of Ephesus. The Abbess, apparently a sensible woman, asks for further details concerning the onset of the madness and then attacks Adriana for her behavior to her husband, claiming that he has become mad because of her everlasting nagging. ". . . thy jealous fits/ Have scared thy husband from the use of wits." Luciana tries to get Adriana to answer the charge, but the shrewish lady announces that she considers the reproof to be deserved, and she resolves to be a changed person in the future. She asks to be allowed to remain in the Priory to nurse her husband. The Abbess, however, refuses to release the supposed Antipholus of Ephesus until he has recovered.

> **COMMENT:** This emphasis on wifely behavior and on the reforma-
> tion of Adriana is unusual in a play of this nature. One expects the
> emphasis in a farce to be totally on the action and not on the de-
> velopment of character and the teaching of behavior. This approach
> prefigures much of Shakespeare's later techniques and attitudes in
> comedy. He can, and does, create developing human beings who
> can engage the emotions as well as the intellect.

Adriana obediently, but sadly, departs. Luciana, however, urges her sister to protest to the Duke about the Abbess. At this moment, the Duke passes by on his way to see the execution of Aegeon, whose day of grace has now expired.

> **COMMENT:** This incident leads us to an understanding of the
> time scheme of the play. All the events take place within a single day.

Adriana falls on her knees before the Duke and tells her story at great length; she requests the Duke to force the Abbess to release her husband. A servant then enters to tell of the escape of Antipholus and Dromio of Ephesus from custody, and they appear almost immediately. Antipholus of Ephesis, himself, then demands justice from the Duke, and tells his side of the story at length. Aegeon thinks he recognizes his son of Syracuse, but he, too, is mistaken. Angelo and the Merchant arrive and bring up the matter of the chain, noting that they had seen it around the neck of the Antipholus who has sought refuge in the Priory. Antipholus of Ephesus denies having the chain, but the Courtezan then identifies her ring, adding that she had seen him enter the Priory. Aegeon announces that the Ephesian pair are his son and servant, but naturally they do not recognize the old man; the Duke corroborates their statement.

Shakespeare now arranges the ultimate confrontation scene with the entrance of the Abbess with Antipholus and Dromio of Syracuse. Immediately, the young man recognizes his father, and to everyone's surprise the Abbess also recognizes Aegeon and repeats the same story that the old man had told at the beginning of the play. She concludes by identifying herself as Aegeon's long-lost wife, Aemilia. After a final round of confused identities, the Antipholi and Dromios are sorted out, various property is returned to its rightful owners, Aegeon is pardoned, and the Abbess invites everyone to a feast where all can catch up on the events of the past thirty-three years.

> **COMMENT:** The Abbess would seem to be in error here. The number mentioned by Aegeon at the beginning of the play was twenty-three years.

SUMMARY: The purpose of this scene is to get a stageful of happy people together and to untangle all the confusions.

1. The identities of the two Antipholi and the two Dromios are finally determined by means of their personal statements, confrontation, and the evidence of the jewelry.

2. The Abbess delivers a homily on wifely conduct to Adriana, who promises to reform.

3. The Abbess identifies herself as Aemilia, the lost wife of Aegeon. Her homily thus turns out to be in the best mother-in-law tradition.

4. Aegeon is pardoned, and the play that began in sorrow now ends in joy with a banquet.

5. Antipholus of Syracuse repeats his declaration of love to Luciana, and everyone is finally paired off.

CHARACTER ANALYSES:
"THE COMEDY OF ERRORS"

In general, the characters of *The Comedy of Errors* are stock types and one can therefore say very little about their character development within the play.

THE TWIN ANTIPHOLI: These are the identical twins of the play, and there is little to distinguish one from the other, except that Antipholus of Ephesus seems to have a shorter temper than his Syracusan twin.

THE TWIN DROMIOS: These are two witty slaves of the play. They generally act in a roguish manner and are frequently beaten by their masters for their saucy comments. They are almost indistinguishable from each other.

ADRIANA: She is the nearest approach to a "round" character in the play. She is a shrew, but, at the same time, some of her shrewishness is justified. She wants equality with men and objects to the strictures that society places upon wives. Nevertheless, she feels affection for Antipholus of Ephesus and is willing to do anything to cure him of his madness, despite the fact that her feelings are hurt because of his apparent disloyalty. She changes in the course of the play and learns some of the rules of matrimonial behavior. After the lecture from the Abbess, she will undoubtedly be a changed character.

LUCIANA: She is a softer character than Adriana, and, whenever her sister rails, she speaks for submissiveness in marriage. She acts as a foil to Adriana, showing up her faults and virtues. However, it is she who urges Adriana to action in trying to get her husband back.

AEGEON: He seems at first to be tragic. He is condemned to death for no fault of his own, and he has led a very sad life as a result of losing a son and his wife. He has very little personality, but is important for relating past events to the present situation.

THE ABBESS: (*Aemilia*): She has a minor role and is primarily the instrument used by Shakespeare to deliver a speech in favor of matrimonial fidelity and behavior. She urges submission on Adriana, and, when her own identity is revealed, she also takes on aspects of the typical mother-in-law.

THE DUKE: He has little that is notable in terms of character. He does, however, seem a trifle inconsistent because he refuses to pardon Aegeon at the beginning, only to do so at the end. Perhaps one may assume that the twin sons will have the money to pay their father's fine.

The other characters are not carefully drawn. They merely have a plot function. This play is basically one of incident, not of character development.

ESSAY QUESTIONS FOR REVIEW: "THE COMEDY OF ERRORS"

1. This play depends largely upon the structure of its action for its fame and its comic effect. How is it constructed?

The Comedy of Errors contains an unexpectedly long introduction or frame narrative in which Aegeon recounts the events which preceded the opening of the play. The first scene, therefore, serves the purpose of dramatic exposition. At the same time, the sad tale of the old man gives depth to what is essentially a farce and it indicates qualities that Shakespeare later added to comedy—sympathy and humanity.

The action of the play is based largely upon one dramatic device, *mistaken identity*. The two sets of twins are constantly confused so that almost all the mathematical possibilities of variation on this general theme are exhausted. The weak point in the plot, however, lies in the fact that the two Syracusans do not understand sooner what is happening since they do know of the existence of their twin brothers while their Ephesian counterparts do not.

There is also a rudimentary subplot in which questions of matrimonial behavior are discussed. The possibility of a match between Antipholus of Syracuse and Luciana is also raised at the end. This subplot undoubtedly is employed for the sake of symmetry so that the twins may be paired off in the final recognition scene.

The final reconciliation and recognition is accomplished by means of coincidence and also confrontation. Both of the twins are wearing jewels which help to establish their identities. The appearance of the Abbess and her identification as the long-lost wife of Aegeon is pure coincidence, while the happy ending with the reprieve of Aegeon is a conventional requirement for such a farce.

2. What are the different attitudes towards marriage found in this play?

Basically, there are three different attitudes towards marriage in this play. The first is that of Adriana, who is slightly suspicious of her husband's fidelity. As a result, she believes in keeping a very close eye on him. She continually upbraids him for being late for dinner and accuses him of misconduct with the Courtezan. She actually has planted ideas of infidelity in his mind, and, when he is angry at being locked out of his house, he threatens unfaithfulness. Similarly, the second attitutde, that of Antipholus of Ephesus, seems to be based also on suspicion and is one in which corporal punishment is thought necessary to control a wife.

The third attitude is one that is shared by Luciana, Adriana's sister, and the Abbess (who turns out to be Adriana's mother-in-law). They both believe it is the duty of a wife to submit to her husband and to avoid nagging him. Luciana counsels moderation, in a very quiet manner, but the Abbess upbraids Adriana, telling her that she has caused her husband's alleged madness by her continual shrewishness. Consequently, Adriana comes to understand that kindness and gentleness rule a husband better than a sharp tongue.

3. What kind of characters are there in this play? Are they types or are they well-developed?

On the whole, the characters of this play are the usual *stock characters* of Plautine comedy. We have the Senex in the old man, Aegeon, the witty slaves in the two Dromios, and the slightly immoral men-about-town in the two Antipholi. These characters exist almost entirely through their actions, which are always shown within the framework of active farce.

There are, however, three other characters which contain the rudiments of development: The three women. Of them, Adriana is the only one who shows any change of character or personality in the course of the play. She is a shrew, yet, at the same time, one has a certain amount of sympathy for her, because she is, indeed, badly used. By the end of the play, her shrewish attitude and sharp tongue are both softened by her experience so that she seems altogether a different person. Both the Abbess and Luciana, in possessing a common attitude towards marriage and being the mouthpieces for their belief, go beyond the realm of the usual one-dimensional characters in a farce.

THE TAMING OF THE SHREW

THE PLAY: This play probably comes directly after *The Comedy of Errors* and is usually dated 1593-94. It, too, deals mainly with middle-class persons and is also a farce with emphasis on action. Nevertheless, Shakespeare has included considerable psychological development for his main character, Katharina, the shrew. Her taming is not achieved in the old way by beating, but through a careful plan aimed at making Katharina herself realize the uselessness of her behavior. Shakespeare has also emphasized differing standards of conduct for husbands and wives, and for maidens as well. In this way, he has also achieved unity, because the main plot of Katharina and Petruchio is reflected in the subplot of Bianca and Lucentio and two different standards of behavior in wooing and wedding are illustrated.

SOURCES AND TEXT: The play, as we know it, first appeared in the First Folio of 1623. But in 1594, an anonymous play called *The Taming of a Shrew* was printed, and reprinted twice more in 1596 and 1607. The relationship of this play to Shakespeare's is by no means clear. The main source is, therefore, not settled; but, for the subplot, the ultimate source is *I Suppositi, The Supposes,* of the Italian poet, Ariosto. Shakespeare thus introduces elements of Italian comedy into his reworking of a traditional farcical theme—the taming of a shrew.

THE PLOT: The play begins with an Induction, a frame narrative in which Christopher Sly, the drunken tinker, is picked up by a Lord, dressed in fine clothes, and made to believe that he has been asleep for years. Sly and a Page, whom he believes to be his wife, then sit down to watch a performance by a group of strolling players who play *The Taming of the Shrew*. After the initial scene of the play proper, Sly disappears.

Baptista Minola, a gentleman of Padua, has two daughters: the elder, Katharina, noted for her scolding and her shrewishness; and the younger, Bianca, equally noted for her gentleness and obedience. Bianca has suitors, Gremio, an old man, and Hortensio while Katharina has none. As a result, Baptista decides to remove Bianca from society until Kate is married. In the course of this scene, Lucentio, a young man from Pisa, sees Bianca and falls desperately in love with her. Gremio and Hortensio then join forces to get Katharina a husband. When Petruchio, a friend of Hortensio, arrives in Padua looking for a wife, they tell him about Kate's shrewishness, but also about her money. Petruchio immediately decides to have her. In the meantime, Lucentio has changed clothes with Tranio, his servant, in order to become a tutor in literature to Bianca, persuading Gremio to sponsor him. Similarly, Hortensio disguises himself as a tutor in music and gets Petruchio to promise to introduce him as such to Baptista. Then Gremio, Hortensio, and Tranio (disguised as Lucentio) offer to pay Petruchio's wooing expenses so that they may be free to woo Bianca.

After a scene in which both Kate's shrewishness and also the gross favoritism of Baptista towards Bianca are shown, all the suitors enter. Petruchio opens proceedings by asking after Katharina; then he presents Hortensio as a music master for Bianca. Gremio presents the disguised Lucentio as a literature master for Bianca, and Biondello presents books for Bianca on behalf of Tranio (disguised as Lucentio). All the gifts are accepted and Petruchio and Baptista are left alone to discuss the financial arrangements of the young man's marriage to Kate. Baptista suggests that Petruchio ask the young lady himself. Petruchio does so in a very stormy wooing scene during which Kate raises her hand to Petruchio, who, being a gentleman, does not hit back. He then claims that Kate has gladly consented and that the wedding day will be next Sunday when the assembled gentlemen return.

Bianca's suitors now commence to bargain with Baptista and they offer him money. Tranio (disguised as Lucentio) offers the most and Baptista accepts him for Bianca with the proviso that "Lucentio's" father ratify the agreement. If not, then Gremio is the chosen candidate. Tranio then goes out to seek a father, the "supposed Vincentio." Bianca's suitors are also shown wooing, and it is obvious that the real Lucentio (disguised as Cambio) is the favorite.

Katharina's wedding day arrives and Petruchio, the bridegroom, is extremely late. When he finally arrives, he is dressed very shabbily and is riding a broken-down horse. He refuses to change his clothes and horrifies everybody in the church by his irreverent behavior. On his return to Baptista's house, he refuses to allow Kate to stay for her own wedding feast and tells her that he now has complete control over her. When they arrive at his country house, he refuses to allow her to eat, drink, sleep, or buy clothes from a tailor he has commissioned. He beats his servants and does not give Katharina food until she is polite.

In the meantime, Lucentio's suit of Bianca is progressing well, and Tranio has managed to find an elderly pedant to be "supposed Vincentio." The Pedant is schooled to tell Baptista that he ratifies whatever arrangement his son "Lucentio" has made with regard to Bianca. This is done, and we discover that the real Lucentio (disguised as Cambio) has made arrangements to marry Bianca secretly.

Petruchio and Katharina then set out for Padua; they meet the real Vincentio, father to Lucentio, and the newlyweds indulge in another session of argumentation until Kate decides that the easiest way out is to appear to agree with her husband.

Finally, in the last act, everyone is confused by the disguised persons, but when the identities are finally sorted out a triple wedding feast is held. Baptista is reconciled to Bianca's marriage which was performed without his consent, and Hortensio has married a wealthy widow. After a discussion, an obedience test is arranged for the three wives. Both the Widow and Bianca refuse to obey their husbands, but Kate obeys; then she lectures the other wives on their duty.

DETAILED SUMMARY OF
"THE TAMING OF THE SHREW"

INDUCTION: SCENE 1

This scene takes place in front of an alehouse on a heath. The Hostess of the alehouse enters with Christopher Sly and demands payment for the glasses he has broken. Sly refuses to pay and the Hostess leaves to get the police; Sly simply curls up and falls asleep.

> **COMMENT:** The purpose of the Induction is frequently debated. At first, it is a realistic English framework for a play set in Italy. For some unexplained reason, Shakespeare drops the rumbunctious Sly after I.i.259. The frame induction was larger in *The Taming of A Shrew.*

The sound of horns is heard and the Lord, who has been hunting, appears with his company to see Sly lying in a durnken stupor. The Lord, noting the swinishness of the man, decides to take Sly, dress him as a lord, and then see whether, on awakening, the tinker will forget his past and accept the new identity offered him. Sly is carried out and the players enter. The Lord greets them in a manner that foreshadows Hamlet's greeting to the players; then he sends them to the buttery for a drink. In addition, the Lord gives orders to a page to dress as a woman and pretend that he is Sly's wife when the drunkard awakens.

SUMMARY: This scene is the opening of the frame narration of the play.

1. Sly argues with the Hostess and then falls into a drunken sleep.

2. The Hostess goes for the police.

3. The Lord decides to dupe Sly into thinking he is of noble rank and works out the details of the deception.

4. The players arrive and are well treated.

INDUCTION: SCENE 2

This scene takes place on the upper stage of the theatre which represents a bedchamber. Sly wakens and calls for ale, but the servants suggest a cup of sack (sherry).

> **COMMENT:** This distinction between the tinker's desire for ale and the servant's suggestion of sack indicates Sly's lack of aristocratic taste despite his newly gained aristocratic clothing.

Sly remains unreformed and calls for the food and drink that he knows. He insists on his identity as Christopher Sly, but gradually with the sound of music and the continual suggestions of the plotters, he comes to accept his new identity. He even seems to believe that he has been asleep for fifteen years and that his wife has been weeping for him. When the disguised page comes to him, Sly immediately asks him into bed, but a messenger arrives announcing that the players have prepared a play. This pleasant comedy has notable medicinal qualities. Sly agrees to watch it.

> **COMMENT:** Shakespeare is here introducing his own play with praise. We are involved in an interesting dramatic device because as the audience, we are watching a play about the presentation of a play. The playwright also gives us some idea of the tonic qualities of comedy.

SUMMARY: Christopher Sly is a man of coarse clay and is proud of that fact. When he awakens he is hard to convince, but he decides to accept his good fortune and his new identity as a lord. The players then arrive to present the play itself.

ACT I: SCENE 1

This scene takes place in a public place in Padua, apparently at a time contemporary with Shakespeare. Lucentio and his man Tranio enter. We find that, like many young men of his day, Lucentio is educating himself by travel and attendance at the university. Consequently, he has come to Padua.

> **COMMENT:** The university in Padua was one of the most famous in Italy in Shakespeare's time. Note that the playwright's knowledge of Italian geography seems weak. He places Padua in the wrong Italian state and erroneously refers to it as a seaport.

Tranio quite wisely warns his master against spending all his time studying philosophy to the exclusion of the arts of love.

At this moment, Baptista Minola and his daughters, Katharina and Bianca, enter. Gremio, an old man, and Hortensio, a young man, both suitors to Bianca, follow. Baptista announces that he will not bestow his younger daughter in marriage until he has obtained a husband for the elder. He offers both of them leave to court Katharina, but both refuse. Katharina objects strenuously to the way in which her father is trying to get rid of her. Hortensio says that she needs to be gentler in order to get a husband, a remark which sends Kate into an angry fit. Bianca says nothing.

> **COMMENT:** This opening scene shows the contrasting characters of Kate and Bianca. It also illustrates the way in which Baptista treats marriage as a bargaining situation.

Tranio then comments on the madness of Kate; Lucentio is overwhelmed with the "mild behaviour and sobriety" of Bianca. Baptista tells Bianca to go inside; Kate makes a cross remark, but Bianca makes a humble speech of obedience before she leaves. Gremio, the elderly suitor, protests against Baptista's decision. The father says that he will employ tutors for Bianca until he will allow her courtship. Kate, after a show of opposition, finally follows Baptista away. Gremio and Hortensio then decide that they will have to work together to obtain a husband for Kate so they will be free to woo Bianca.

> **COMMENT:** This scene exposes Katharina as a young woman who is constantly in opposition to those around her, while Bianca obeys sweetly. The plot to find a husband for Kate heightens her undesirability as a wife.

Lucentio, during this time, has been so overwhelmed by the beauty of Bianca that he has not even noticed Kate. When he hears of Baptista's plan to remove Bianca from society until Kate is married, Lucentio decides to disguise himself as a schoolmaster and get himself placed in Baptista's household as a tutor to Bianca. In the meantime, Tranio will disguise himself as Lucentio.

> **COMMENT:** This section of the play, the subplot, is taken from the Italian comedy *I Suppositi,* translated into English by George Gascoigne as *The Supposes*. It is based on a series of disguises.

At this point, Biondello, another of Lucentio's servants, enters to see Tranio dressed as his master. Lucentio makes up a story about having killed a man and therefore having to disguise himself in order to escape.

Suddenly, we return to Sly, who has been watching the play all along. He nods, but when asked if he enjoys the play he replies " 'Tis a very excellent piece of work, madam lady: would 'twere done!" And that is his last appearance.

SUMMARY: The opening scene of this play is extremely important for its exposition:

1. It introduces the principal characters in the play and indicates the behavior that will characterize them throughout the action.

2. Baptista is shown as a shrewd man who plays favorites and drives a hard bargain in matrimonial negotiations.

3. Katherina reveals herself as a young woman who opposes everyone and likes to hear her own voice.

4. Bianca is shown in every way to be her opposite. She is a foil who emphasizes all Kate's disadvantages.

5. The situation of the announced wooers, Hortensio and old Gremio, is made clear.

6. Lucentio is shown as falling immediately in love with Bianca in a highly romantic, sudden manner.

7. The subplot of the wooing of Bianca begin once Hortensio and Gremio join forces; Lucentio decides to disguise himself as a tutor.

8. The organized search for a husband for Kate begins.

ACT I: SCENE 2

This scene takes place in Padua in front of Hortensio's house. Petruchio is talking to his servant Grumio when he flies into a rage at the stupidity of his man and beats him roundly.

> **COMMENT:** Here we have much the same relationship between master and servant as in the farce, *The Comedy of Errors,* in which servants are frequently beaten.

Hortensio then enters to greet his old friend Petruchio; he tries to make up the quarrel between master and servant. The misunderstanding is resolved.

> **COMMENT:** Grumio is like the Dromios of *The Comedy of Errors* because he mistakes the word, sometimes by accident, and sometimes on purpose.

Petruchio, in answer to a question from Hortensio, tells his friend that, since his father is dead, he is now traveling in search of a wealthy wife. Hortensio has the glimmering of a superb idea—he tells Petruchio that he has a candidate. The young man says that he does not care about looks, age, disposition, or anything—except money. Hortensio continues; he tells his cynical friend about Katharina, that she has money, and that she is a renowned shrew. Petruchio replies that he'll marry her anyway, just as long as she has money, and says that he knows of her family as well. Grumio comments that Petruchio's evil disposition would seem to make him more than a match for Kate.

> **COMMENT:** Petruchio is shown to be a cynical young man lacking in patience. *His wish to marry for money is not to be taken as a fault. He is really the only person in the entire play who is honest enough to admit his motives.* All the other wooers, with the possible exception of Lucentio, are out for money. Baptista is not exempt from this general accusation.

Hortensio then asks Petruchio, in return for the information, to present him in disguise as a tutor in music to Bianca. Gremio then brings in Lucentio, disguised as Cambio—a literature tutor for Bianca. The old man's heart rejoices when Hortensio introduces Petruchio as the man who "Will undertake to woo curst Katharine . . ." and, further, to marry her if her dowry is sufficient.

> **COMMENT:** It was, and in some places still is, the custom that the bride's father give a dowry, a sum of money to the bridegroom. Should the husband die, the wife is entitled to the amount of the dowry plus money from her husband's estate, her jointure.

Gremio is impressed with Petruchio who claims that he is not afraid of anything Kate might do. Tranio, disguised as Lucentio, enters with Biondello and says that he, too, is a suitor for Bianca's hand. He praises the younger daughter, but Petruchio expresses interest only in Kate. Hortensio, Gremio, and the disguised Tranio all offer to finance Petruchio's wooing so that they may compete freely for Bianca.

SUMMARY: This scene really completes the exposition of the plot; it also advances the subplot.

1. It introduces the last of the major characters, Petruchio, and shows him a merry, cynical, fortune hunter.

2. It reveals the plans of Bianca's suitors:
a. Hortensio will disguise himself as a music master.
b. Lucentio will disguise himself as a literature teacher.

3. It forces all Bianca's suitors to declare a truce and cooperate in Petruchio's wooing of Kate.

ACT II: SCENE 1

This entire act is comprised of one scene which takes place in a room in the house of Baptista Minola in Padua. It begins with Bianca, whose hands are tied behind her back, begging for mercy from Katharina. She offers to do anything Kate wishes, since she knows her duty to her elders. But, in response to Kate's questions, she swears that she has not "yet beheld that special face" among her suitors which she would prefer to all others. Baptista then enters and upbraids Kate for her cruelty to her meek sister. In anger, Kate rushes after Bianca who exits. Kate then turns on Baptista; she accuses him of favoritism and claims that she "must dance bare-foot" on Bianca's wedding day, and "for your love to her lead apes in hell."

> **COMMENT:** These possibilities are statements of popular custom and belief. If a younger sister married before the elder, in order to avoid spinsterhood, the elder girl must dance barefoot at the wedding. "Leading apes in hell" was considered the eternal fate of an old maid. In making these comments, Kate reveals her own frustrations. Her father is not making any effort to find her a husband, except in a negative sense, and she is continually being reproached for not being like her sister. Small wonder that she is angry and shrewish. Bianca's sweetness must indeed be cloying.

Gremio, accompanied by the disguised Lucentio, Petruchio with the disguised Hortensio, and Tranio with Biondello carrying books and a lute, all enter. Petruchio immediately inquires after Kate. Baptista hedges. Petruchio continues in praise of Katharina's beauty, virtue, and wit, and asks to meet her. He then offers Hortensio as a tutor to Bianca; Gremio introduces the disguised Lucentio as a tutor in Greek, Latin, and languages.

Tranio then presents himself as a suitor for Bianca and offers some books for her edification. The suitors are sent away and Baptista and Petruchio get down to business.

The conversation between Petruchio and Baptista concerns money. Petruchio says he is in a hurry. After stating his own financial position he comes straight to the point: "What dowry shall I have with her to wife?" Baptista offers one half of his lands after his death and twenty thousand crowns immediately. Petruchio offers in return to assure Kate of a share in all his lands and leases should she be left a widow. He then very shrewdly suggests that written documents be drawn up in order to ensure that the terms of the contracts will be fulfilled.

> **COMMENT:** This businesslike approach was a common one in the sixteenth century. It was important for a young man to marry money, and for a young girl to have her financial security arranged. The wealthy and noble classes in Elizabethan England, for example, were frequently more interested in the financial arrangements than in the amours of marriage. Note that Baptista does not haggle and he does not try to get more money out of Petruchio. He simply wants Kate off his hands.

Baptista then says that he wants Petruchio to obtain Kate's love, "for that is all in all."

> **COMMENT:** Somehow, these words do not ring quite true. Perhaps Baptista is safeguarding himself by wanting Petruchio to know exactly what kind of bad bargain he is getting. Otherwise, there is a faint possibility that Petruchio could refuse to fulfill the contract, and indeed, even to marry Kate.

Petruchio confidently replies that he expects no trouble "For I am rough and woo not like a babe." Baptista, rather skeptically, wishes him good luck, and his doubts seem to be justified when Hortensio enters with a bleeding head, complaining that Kate has just broken a lute over it. The exasperated Baptista leaves and Kate enters. Petruchio immediately begins to woo her, using the exact approach that she herself has been using elsewhere in the play. He opposes her in every possible way and praises her for the qualities she lacks in abundance (II.i.244-253). He praises her gentleness, her courtesy, and slowness in speech while Kate rails more and more loudly at him.

> **COMMENT:** The virtues that Petruchio praises in Kate are those that the Elizabethans truly desired their women to possess. At this point in the play, of course, it is Bianca who embodies such ideal virtues rather than Kate.

Kate threatens him with violence, and indeed strikes him, but Petruchio refuses to reply in kind because he is a gentleman. But then he announces "And will you, nill you, I will marry you." He further tells her that he alone is a suitable husband for her, "For I am he am born to tame you,

Kate." He concludes with a determination to take Katharina for his wife.

> **COMMENT:** Petruchio is indeed right and it would appear that Katharina in part agrees with him. He is the first man whom she has not scared off with her shrewish disposition. Further, Petruchio is a handsome and intriguing young man.

With the return of Baptista, Gremio, and Tranio, Katharina grumbles about the match; Petruchio gives a hilariously incorrect account of the wooing, claiming that Kate has acted precisely as a well-mannered, quiet, and charming young lady is expected to. He announces that the wedding is set for Sunday, and, at the same time, he seems to hit on the truth about Kate: "If she be curst, it is for policy."

> **COMMENT:** Petruchio is correct here. As the play progresses, we will see that Katharina is a mettlesome girl of spirit who is usually overlooked in favor of quiet, smug little Bianca. As a result, Kate can assert her individuality only by openly opposing all those who despise her and praise insipidity.

Baptista is overjoyed. A difficult daughter is off his hands. He has the betrothed join hands, and the equally happy wooers of Bianca act as witnesses in this public engagement ceremony.

> **COMMENT:** These proceedings are a very precise parallel with Elizabethan matrimonial practice. The couple express in words their desire to marry, they join hands before witnesses, and sometimes exchange rings. Finally, they kiss.

After the departure of Katharina and Petruchio, the wooers of Bianca approach Baptista. Note that here Baptista does not think of asking Bianca's consent, and that his approach is quite different from the way in which he arranged Kate's match. He now has more than one wooer; consequently, he runs an affair not unlike an auction by asking each wooer to bid against the other.

> **COMMENT:** Obviously, Baptista is more concerned with money that with love in marriage, because Signior Gremio is too old to be a pleasant match for Bianca.

Gremio opens the bidding by offering all he owns, but is outbid by Tranio (disguised as Lucentio) who offers his father's property as well. Gremio admits he is beaten so Baptista accepts the higher bid, but, as a shrewd bargainer, he leaves himself covered. The supposed Lucentio's father must ratify the offer, and if he will not, then Gremio will be the accepted suitor. Tranio, in a final soliloquy, remarks that he must find a man who will pretend to be his father. "Supposed Lucentio" needs to find a father, "Supposed Vincentio."

SUMMARY: This scene manages to get almost all the major incidents of the plot and the subplot well on their way.

1. It has Petruchio woo Katarina, both in financial terms and in personal contact with the girl.

2. It introduces us to the tactics Petruchio is going to use in the future to tame his "wild Kate."

3. It hints at the reason for Katharina's shrewish behavior.

4. The wild opposition of the wooing of Katharina and Petruchio points forward to further madness at the wedding.

5. It illustrates two aspects of marriage for money. Baptista is so glad to get rid of Kate that he does not bargain. But, when he has more than one suitor, he unashamedly auctions Bianca off to the highest bidder.

6. The contrast between Kate and Bianca is further developed. Kate beats Bianca who tries desperately to gain her approval. Baptista seems a trifle afraid of Kate because he insists on Petruchio's talking personally with the girl, but he arranges Bianca's marriage without consultation with her. Apparently, he can rely upon her obedience.

7. Shakespeare may here be making fun of some of the typical matrimonial customs among the wealthy of his day. Money is more important than love.

ACT III: SCENE 1

This scene takes place a short time later in the house of Baptista. Hortensio and Lucentio are instructing Bianca, and it is not long before we discover that Lucentio is telling her of his love, under cover of translating from Latin. Hortensio tries very hard to interest Bianca in his lute and his music, and he presents her with a poem. Bianca, however, refuses it.

COMMENT AND SUMMARY: This brief scene shows us that Bianca is rather a sly minx. She plays one wooer off against the other and carefully avoids committing herself. Her behavior here casts doubt on the sincerity of her humble and obedient demeanor. On the whole, Kate emerges as more honest than her sister.

ACT III: SCENE 2

This scene takes place on Sunday, Kate's wedding day, outside Baptista's house. Everything is ready for the marriage, Kate is dressed, but Petruchio is nowhere to be found. The bride is almost beside herself with angry frustration from the blow to her pride. Tranio counsels patience, an ironic suggestion to the impatient Katharina. Finally, Kate leaves, weeping, and, for once, even Baptista cannot blame her.

    COMMENT: This is Petruchio's first victory. He has reduced Kate to tears, and further, he makes her less able to resist him later on.

Biondello then rushes in to say that Petruchio is coming, but that he is dressed in the most appalling collection of old clothes, and is riding with half-mended harness on a broken-down old horse. Petruchio rushes in almost immediately and calls for Kate, brushing aside all hints that he should change his clothes: "To me she's married, not unto my clothes." Tranio, however, makes an astute comment: "He hath some meaning in his mad attire."

> **COMMENT:** Petruchio is humiliating Kate further by refusing to change into decent attire. He is also "softening her up." At the same time, he knows that her pride will not let her back down at this point. He definitely has a reason for his boorish behavior. Kate is not marrying anyone except the real Petruchio, and she must learn what he is like.

As everyone departs for the wedding, Tranio and Lucentio speak about their plans to have Lucentio marry Bianca. In desperation about the difficulties facing him, Lucentio says that it might be a better idea to elope and marry secretly.

> **COMMENT:** We seem to gather more evidence that Bianca is less obedient than she at first seemed. The very fact that Lucentio suggests an elopement without Baptista's consent would seem to indicate at least the possibility that Bianca might agree. And, as we learn later, she does.

Just at this point, old Signior Gremio appears to detail to the characters in the play (and the audience) the way in which Petruchio has just made an utter shambles of the marriage ceremony by answering the priest's questions by swearing, by stamping around, by drinking the ceremonial wine as if he were carousing, by throwing the wine-soaked cakes at the sexton, and lastly, by kissing the bride with a resounding smack, instead of a politely religious peck. Kate is, of course, afraid, and Petruchio has gained more advantage of her.

The wedding party returns from the church and Petruchio announces that, although a wedding feast is generally expected, he and Katharina must leave immediately. His wife entreats him to stay, but Petruchio is adamant. For the first time, these two are openly crossing swords and Katharina, true to form, defies Petruchio, loses her temper, and resists. At this moment, Petruchio intervenes, and, acting as if he were being attacked by the assembled company, he announces that he is Kate's master. He then proceeds to state exactly the extent of his power over her as his wife. And, legally, she is entirely within his power. He draws his sword and orders Grumio to do the same, claiming that they are to be attacked. Since he meets with no opposition he leaves with Kate and his servant.

> **COMMENT:** This is Petruchio's first public victory over Kate. She does not answer for two reasons: (1) she is too frightened; and (2) Petruchio has stated his legal power over her correctly. His statement sums up the legal rights of an Elizabethan husband over his wife.

The wedding feast proceeds without Kate, and Bianca sits in the place of honor.

SUMMARY: This scene is important for its bearing on the future matrimonial conduct of Petruchio and Katharina, as well as on the Bianca subplot.

1. Petruchio deliberately keeps Kate waiting until she is tearfully certain that he will not come to marry her. As a result, she pays little attention to his eccentric dress when he finally appears.

2. The angry behavior of Petruchio during the ceremony makes her so sick with fear that she does not remonstrate with him.

3. Although she crosses Petruchio in public, he does not let her get away with such defiant behavior. He carefully states her legal situation; therefore, she has to follow him.

4. Petruchio's actions at the wedding feast are nominally dictated by love for her; therefore she cannot defy him.

5. The character of Bianca is shown to be rather sly and secretive. She toys with her wooers and appears to plot with them. She is by no means the paragon of obedience that Baptista thinks.

ACT IV: SCENE 1

This scene takes place in Petruchio's country house just after the wedding of Petruchio and Katharina. Grumio enters and calls for preparations because the master is about to arrive. He tells of the fantastic occurrences during the journey from Padua and the way in which the entire journey seems to have been one long accident: "how she prayed, that never prayed before," and how Kate tried to come between Petruchio and his wrath in beating Grumio.

> **COMMENT:** Throughout the entire play, Petruchio never raises his hand to Kate, although he seems to hit almost everyone else within range. His mindless rage is a deliberate parody of Kate's own, and it is by showing Katharina the stupidity of her own behavior that Petruchio is finally able to reform her—as far as he wishes.

When Petruchio enters, he shouts for his servants and complains that preparations have not been made for them. He hits at the servants who seem to him to be moving too slowly until Kate remonstrates with him. When the mutton arrives, Petruchio rejects it as being burnt, and, in answer to Kate's comments, says that burnt meat is bad for the choleric temper of them both.

> **COMMENT:** This is a reference to one of the four major humours (body fluids) of Elizabethan psychology. *Choler* was the humour that caused anger if possessed to excess, and, since the only way to

regulate the balance of fluids was by means of the diet, a choleric person ought to avoid all foods that might cause choler. Therefore, Petruchio is looking after Kate's well-being as well as his own.

The servants see precisely what he is doing: "He kills her in her own humour." Then, while Kate is undressing for bed, Petruchio explains his policy: he plans to reform Kate by refusing to allow her to eat, or to sleep, until she changes her disposition. But he plans to give the impression that all these actions are "done in reverend care of her." In this way, he is drawing Kate's claws. "This is a way to kill a wife with kindness."

COMMENTARY AND SUMMARY: This scene reveals the way Petruchio plans to tame his shrew. It is important to note that he always seems to have Kate's welfare in mind. Also, much of the taming takes place off stage. Shakespeare is broadening the play from a knockabout farce into a play that possesses psychological depth.

ACT IV: SCENE 2

This scene occurs in Padua before Baptista's house. Tranio and Hortensio are discussing the progress of their wooing of Bianca. Hortensio is disturbed that Bianca is interested in neither of them and suggests that they observe Bianca's behavior. Tranio, the supposed Lucentio, claims that Bianca loves Lucentio only. At that point, Bianca enters and we find that he is right. The real Lucentio, disguised as Cambio, is teaching the girl "the art to love." On seeing this, Tranio declares that he will give up the girl entirely, and Hortensio says that he will do the same, and what is more, he will marry a wealthy widow who has been pursuing him for some time.

> **COMMENT:**   Hortensio's plan shows us that he has always been out for money in his marriage. Since widows had complete control of their money, they were always good marital prospects for ambitious young men in Elizabethan England. The duplicity of Bianca becomes more obvious.

At this point, the Pedant arrives and Tranio, after frightening him with his supposed danger in Padua, persuades him to pretend that he is Signior Vincentio, the father of Lucentio.

SUMMARY: This scene is important primarily for the advancement of the subplot:

1. Bianca, in encouraging Lucentio, is shown to be following her own heart rather than her father's will.

2. Hortensio thinks that he has convinced Tranio (the supposed Lucentio) of Bianca's infidelity to him. Both men forswear her.

3. Hortensio announces his intention of marrying a wealthy widow for her "kindness," although one suspects that her money is also important.

4. Tranio (the supposed Lucentio) acquires a father, "Supposed Vincentio."

ACT IV: SCENE 3

This scene takes place in a room in Petruchio's house. Kate is hungry, tired, desperate, and exasperated beyond measure. But Petruchio always acts in the name of perfect love for her; therefore she cannot be angry. Even the servant, Grumio, tantalizes her with promises of food, but Petruchio will not let her eat until she acts civilly towards him. As a reward, he tells her that he has arranged for a tailor to bring her some new clothes. Then he finds fault with everything and runs counter to everything Kate says, so that, finally, she gets no new clothes. Instead, Petruchio lectures her on the riches of the mind as opposed to riches shown in dress. This scene was deliberately staged by Petruchio, because he has Hortensio to pay the tailor for his trouble. The new bridegroom then suggests that they all return to Padua to visit Baptista.

COMMENT AND SUMMARY: This scene is meant to show the progress of Kate's taming, or rather her re-education. Petruchio brings her to heel by refusing to allow her to eat, drink, sleep, or buy new clothes until she is polite. In his attacks on the tailor, he forces Kate to intercede for someone else once again, and, in his speech on the folly of clothes, he tries to teach her to look for an inward reality rather than an outward appearance. Note how Shakespeare alternates plot and subplot in order to bring both to a conclusion in the next act.

ACT IV: SCENE 4

This scene takes place in Padua outside Baptista's house. The Pedant (Supposed Vincentio), asks Baptista for the hand of Bianca for his son Lucentio and he ratifies the earlier agreement. Baptista, however, wants the financial contract drawn up in writing. He wants to sign it elsewhere so that he can keep Signior Gremio in reserve in case the match should fall through. At this point, Baptista sends Cambio, the disguised Lucentio, to tell Bianca that "she's like to be Lucentio's wife." Indeed, she is, but not in the sense Baptista expects.

> **COMMENT:** Baptista outfoxes himself here because of his greed. It is only now that Bianca is informed of the marriage negotiations. Again, Baptista claims to have noticed affection between Bianca and the supposed Lucentio, something of which the audience is ignorant.

Biondello and the real Lucentio then discuss the way they will deceive Baptista and we find that a priest is ready to perform a secret marriage immediately. Lucentio needs only to take his bride and witnesses with him for the ceremony.

COMMENT AND SUMMARY: This would be a legal marriage, and Baptista has given his consent to it, only he has accepted the wrong Lucentio. Bianca, we see now, acts without Baptista's knowledge, and, as we learn later in the play, she is almost as independent as Kate.

ACT IV: SCENE 5

This scene takes place on the public road. Kate, Petruchio, and Hortensio are journeying to Padua when Petruchio remarks on the brilliance of the moon. Kate contradicts him by saying it is the sun, and she is right. But Petruchio becomes so enraged that Kate follows Hortensio's advice and agrees with him. Immediately, Petruchio says the opposite, that the sun is shining, and Kate wearily tells him it can be whatever he wants to be as far as she is concerned.

> **COMMENT:** This interchange reveals that for the first time Petruchio agrees with something Katharina has said. By now, Kate is beginnning to see the joke in this continual opposition to her.

At this moment, the real Vincentio enters and Petruchio immediately addresses him as a young gentlewoman. Kate replies in kind, and out-does Petruchio in praising the beauty of the "young lady." He comes right back at her and says that she is looking at an old man, but Kate recovers brilliantly by turning the tables on Petruchio saying that her eyes "have been so bedazzled with the sun," an allusion to the previous exchange. This remark now alerts Petruchio to the fact that Kate now understands his game.

> **COMMENT:** Possibly, Kate would sound a trifle uncertain as she says the word "sun," in order to joke at Petruchio's expense. She is just as witty as he is, but rather than cross him, she is now pre-pared to play his game, as he has done with her.

SUMMARY: This scene represents Kate's capitulation. Nevertheless, she does not become a passive creature. She has learned to control her tongue and to consider other people. As for Petruchio, he is merry over their mutual joking.

ACT V: SCENE 1

This scene takes place in Padua in front of Lucentio's house. The real Lucentio runs off to church to marry Bianca, while Gremio wonders where the young man might be. Petruchio, Vincentio, Grumio, and their attendants come in and a merry display of confusion takes place when the disguised persons meet the real ones. The spectacle reaches its height with the arrival of the newly married Bianca and Lucentio. Kate and Petruchio enjoy themselves hugely; Baptista realizes that Bianca has de-ceived him. All are soon reconciled, however, and Petruchio asks Kate for a kiss. She roguishly plays the role of modest matron and says that she is ashamed to kiss in public. Petruchio again threatens to return to his home with her, so she kisses him willingly.

SUMMARY: This scene unties all the confusion of the supposes, or disguises. The real Vincentio is identified; the real Lucentio reveals himself; Baptista discovers the real nature of Bianca, because she has married secretly and, in a sense, against his will. The real nature of Kate is also revealed—she has indeed been curst merely for policy.

ACT V: SCENE 2

This last scene of the play takes place in a room in Lucentio's house, and it represents a gay feast at which every one of the major characters is present. All three married couples are there: Petruchio and Kate, Lucentio and Bianca, and Hortensio and his Widow. In the course of conversation the Widow makes a slighting remark about Kate's disposition and Petruchio's marriage to a shrew. Katharina becomes angry, and Petruchio offers to bet that she will overwhelm the Widow in a fight. Even the formerly reticent Bianca gets into the act and makes a couple of jests at Kate's expense.

> **COMMENT:** Note that despite the "taming," Kate will still argue, and even fight, when she thinks herself wronged.

With the departure of the ladies, the gentlemen start comparing the obedience of their wives, and on hearing Baptista's remark that Kate is "the veriest shrew of all," Petruchio wagers her obedience against all comers. The terms are laid down and each husband is to ask, or command, his wife to come to him. The one whose wife obeys most quickly will be the winner. Both Bianca and the Widow refuse to come, but Kate obeys immediately and without question—she is still different from the other women. Petruchio then sends Kate back to fetch the disobedient wives, to thrash them, if necessary. Finally, they return, Bianca and the Widow arguing rather peevishly.

Petruchio has Kate perform another act of obedience by telling her to remove her hat and to stamp on it. Again, she obeys; then Petruchio asks for the ultimate act of obedience—a statement of the duty a woman owes her husband. Kate replies with a speech that extols feminine subordination, since the station and physical capacities of women are different from those of men. She concludes by offering to place her hand under her husband's foot. Petruchio calls for a kiss, and the play concludes with the shrew tamed, although Lucentio is skeptical.

COMMENT AND SUMMARY: Lucentio seems to have seen more clearly than the other what has happened. Kate is tamed, but not crushed. Her final speech is for the benefit of the company, and is a joint joke played on them by Petruchio and her. They have worked out their own way of living together, and Kate has learned how to go along with Petruchio's merry disposition. In this kind of marriage, she no longer needs to assert her independence by shrewish behavior.

CHARACTER ANALYSES:
"THE TAMING OF THE SHREW"

KATHARINA: She is reputed to be a shrew, but in effect this is only her outward appearance. Far from being the stock shrew of medieval or Elizabethan drama, Kate is the first of Shakespeare's witty women, and an independent-minded girl who has discovered that the only way she can preserve her integrity is to oppose what others are saying. Oddly enough, she is obedient to her father in her marriage and fulfills his wishes without apparent reluctance. At the end of the play, she is said to be tamed, but she is certainly not crushed. In some ways, she is as independent as ever, but she has learned when she must keep silent. She possesses a fine sense of humor and can even outdo her husband in carrying a ridiculous situation to its hilarious conclusion. Her final speech does not merely show the complete reformation of Kate. It is a statement of the usual beliefs of the time concerning the position of women in marriage; however she and Petruchio seem to have worked a marriage of mutual give and take.

PETRUCHIO: He is the young man from Verona who says he has "come to wive it wealthily in Padua." Certainly, he does just that, but then he is simply more honest than the other wooers. As a result he gets a wife who is worthy of him. He is lively, impatient, and well suited to Kate. They are two of a kind who woo each other by opposition, and Kate is forced to respect him as the first person she has not been able to cow with her sharp tongue. He manages to tame Kate by making her see the ridiculous nature of her own behavior. Once she gains this self-knowledge she is a fit wife for a Petruchio who would, most probably, have been bored with a predictable woman. Above all, Petruchio is clever, and possesses a sense of fun. He never raises his hand to Kate, although he does have provocation; therefore, he never arouses her enmity. Further, his opposition to Kate's behavior is skillfully based on consideration for his wife. Finally, Kate sees that the joke is on her. By the end of the play, she and Petruchio have learned how to manage each other so that the last test of obedience is really their mutual joke on the assembled company.

BIANCA: At first, one takes her as a sweet, wronged, charming, obedient young girl whose father's word is law. But, as the play progresses, she becomes an accomplished little plotter who is perfectly capable of disobeying her father and marrying secretly. By the end of the play, she is shown to be almost as independent as her sister, but she is less honest about it. She acts as a foil to Kate, showing up her bad points, but then proves to possess some of them herself.

LUCENTIO: He is a typical romantic lover who falls in love at first sight. He is also an adept plotter and able user of disguise to gain his own ends. As a character, he is very lightly drawn.

BAPTISTA: He is the typical father who wants nothing less than complete obedience from his daughters; he wishes to organize their lives entirely. He dislikes his elder daughter because she has enough courage to stand up to him and to want her own way in some things. His insistence on control forces Kate into shrewishness and Bianca into plotting behind his back. He is also concerned with marrying his daughters to money—in fact, that seems to be his sole aim in arranging the marriage of Bianca. He is guilty of favoritism and shows Bianca far more consideration than he does his independent elder daughter. Finally, he outfoxes himself, because Bianca makes a marriage of love, and, although he pushed Kate into the arms of the first suitor to come along, she acquired a decidedly compatible husband.

ESSAY QUESTIONS FOR REVIEW: "THE TAMING OF THE SHREW"

1. Discuss the various attitudes towards marriage shown in this play.

There are three different attitudes toward marriage in this play. The first is that of Katharina and of Petruchio. Each of them wishes to marry a partner who is compatible. At the same time, neither wants to settle for mild-mannered obedience. Petuchio is indeed "born to tame . . . Kate" and she knows that he is not merely her master, but her equal in wit as well.

On the other hand, we have the attitude that is pictured by Baptista, Gremio, and Hortensio, which is that money is all important. To some extent one may say that Petruchio upholds the same attitude because he originally claims that he is interested in Kate only for her money. Nevertheless, his marriage does not seem to succeed merely because of Kate's dowry. Baptista is the most notable exponent of this mercenary attitude, particularly in the scene in which he almost literally auctions Bianca off to the highest bidder. Money is obviously significant so he does not seem remotely disturbed that he is possibly going to allow his daughter to marry a man who is a great deal older than she—just as long as he has sufficient money. Similarly, Hortensio takes care to marry a wealthy widow in order to improve his financial circumstances.

The third attitude is that of Lucentio, and, to a certain extent, of Bianca. They believe in marriage for love. Lucentio falls in love with Bianca at first sight and he woos her in a conventionally romantic manner—in disguise. These two elope and marry secretly without the consent of Baptista. The interesting treatment is that the docile daughter is the one who elopes.

Finally, at the end of the play, Kate speaks in favor of wifely obedience in all things while the Widow who married Hortensio for his looks, and Bianca who married for passion, are both disobedient. The joke is that Kate has actually married a handsome young man for his compatibility with her—underneath their merry war they are really in love.

2. How does Petruchio tame Katharina? Is she really tamed?

Petruchio makes his attempt to bring Kate to his way of thinking by opposing her at every turn and by behaving in an irritating manner similar to her own. He never raises his hand to her, but he beats almost everyone else in sight. As a result, Kate becomes aware of how foolish her behavior is, and she also finds herself defending the persons whom Petruchio attacks and beats. Petruchio also deprives Kate of food and rest until she is almost desperate, but he is not cruel. Certainly not! He takes very great pains that everything he does is done under the guise of perfect love. As a result, Kate has no chance either to reply to him or to get angry with him. He also frightens her with the intensity of his rages so that she is afraid to cross him. This is particularly true at her own wedding when Petruchio not only humiliates her, but also tells her exactly what her legal status is.

Finally, Kate sees that Petruchio is, in effect, playing a series of practical jokes on her, and she strikes back—not with her hands, but with her wit. When Petruchio contradicts her in public, she slyly turns the tables on him by extending his impossible suggestions to their furthest logical point. She has a sense of humor that is equal to that of Petruchio.

By the end of the play, Kate is not actually tamed into complete submission. She and Petruchio have managed to contrive a pleasant way to live together. Her last speech about obedience is their joint joke on the assembled company.

3. How is this play constructed? What kind of play is it?

This humanized farce is based on a main plot—that of Katharina and Petruchio; and a subplot—that of the marriage of Bianca and Lucentio. There is also an Induction regarding the character of Christopher Sly. Sly disappears from the action early in the play. The important organizational device is that of the plot and subplot.

Contrast is the main quality to note in the relationship of the two plots. Whereas the wooing of Petruchio and Katharina is rowdy and merry, that of Lucentio and Bianca is sentimental and sweet. The attributes that Katharina lacks seem to be embodied in Bianca, but, by the end of the play, both of these characters seem to have changed attitudes. Bianca then seems more shrewish than her sister. The subplot is also concerned with many disguises or "supposes," so that a great deal of confusion takes place which complicates the plot.

THE TWO GENTLEMEN OF VERONA

THE PLAY: This play is usually dated 1594-95 and it is important because it possesses many of the elements that Shakespeare later used in other comedies. Some of these elements are: the two contrasting pairs of lovers who appear in most of Shakespeare's comedies; the girl disguised as a page who reappears in *As You Like It* and *Twelfth Night;* the rope ladder which is employed in the source of *Romeo and Juliet;* the young men dying of love who are found in *Much Ado About Nothing, As You Like It,* and *Twelfth Night;* and lastly, the clowns who are the forerunners of those in *Much Ado* and *The Merchant of Venice*. Further, the debate on friendship and love has resemblances to the Sonnets. Shakespeare's power of character depiction has increased, but one difficulty of this play arises because more well-rounded characters than usual are placed in a deliberately unrealistic comedy situation. The two elements do not quite mingle, and when a realistically drawn character acts according to the conventions of stylized comedy the audience tends to object.

SOURCES AND TEXT: Shakespeare seems to have based the play on a pastoral romance *Diana Enamorada* written in Portuguese by Jorge de Montemayor. Probably he saw the later English translation by Bartholomew Yonge. The courtship of Felismena and Don Felix is almost identical to that of Julia and Proteus. There was a lost play *Felix and Philiomena* (acted before Queen Elizabeth in 1584) which may have influenced the playwright. The conflict between friendship and love may also be related to the novel *Euphues,* by the Elizabethan writer, John Lyly, which contains similar discussions.

The first printed text of the play appeared in the First Folio, 1623. It is a fairly good one, but there are some unexplained difficulties, notably the confusion between verse and prose. One theory suggests that the text was "assembled," put together from the individual actors' parts, with the result that some errors were made. Shakespeare's Italian geography again seems odd: Verona, Padua, Mantua, and Milan are jumbled together, and people seem to take a ship to go from Verona to Milan.

THE PLOT: Valentine leaves his friend Proteus in Verona to go to Milan to continue his education at the court of the Duke. Proteus, however, is paralyzed into inactivity by the depth of his passion for Julia; therefore, he stays behind rather than educate himself by travel and experience in another court. After Valentine's departure, Antonio, Proteus' father, decides to send his son to Milan as he is disturbed because the young man is stagnating at home. After bidding Julia a tender farewell, and exchanging rings with her, Valentine leaves. Julia is portrayed as a rather witty young lady who plays with the affections of Proteus, but who, nevertheless, loves him dearly.

When Proteus arrives in Milan he finds that, instead of seeking honor, his friend Valentine has been overcome with love for a lady named Silvia. In fact, Valentine's case is just as bad as his own. But the moment Proteus sees Silvia, he, too, falls desperately in love with her and plots to gain her for himself. When Proteus finds out that the Duke of Milan, Silvia's father, wishes to marry her to Thurio, and that Valentine and Silvia have decided to elope, he interferes. He informs the Duke of Valentine's plot so that his friend will not be able to gain the lady. Proteus has now sinned against the codes of love and friendship. He has forgotten Julia, whose ring he still wears, and he has betrayed the confidence of a friend. Valentine is banished; he flees to the forest where he meets a band of outlaws who elect him their leader.

In the meantime Proteus tries unsuccessfullly to win the loyal Silvia for himself under cover of aiding Sir Thurio, the foolish knight who is Valentine's rival. Then Julia appears disguised as a page because she longs to be with her beloved who, ironically, no longer cares for her. Proteus takes Julia into his service and sends her to woo Silvia for him. Heartbroken, Julia does as she is told, only to be amazed at the loyalty and pity of Silvia who will not grant Proteus' suit. Finally, when Silvia hears that the Duke is going to force her to marry Thurio, she arranges to escape to the forest with Sir Eglamour, a knight sworn to love's service.

Proteus, Thurio, Julia, and the Duke all end up in the forest, and, when Proteus gets Silvia in his power, he attempts to force the unwilling maiden to yield to his will. At this point, Valentine appears and upbraids his disloyal friend, who immediately repents. As a sign of forgiveness, Valentine offers Silvia to Proteus; Julia swoons, and by means of the ring she is wearing she is identified and her lover is repentant. The Duke enters with Thurio who, on being threatened by Valentine, gives up all claims to Silvia. The Duke is angered by Thurio's cowardice and consents to the marriage of Valentine and Silvia. Valentine then suggests a double wedding and asks the Duke's pardon for the outlaw band. The play thus ends happily with the wrongs done to both love and friendship righted.

DETAILED SUMMARY OF
"THE TWO GENTLEMEN OF VERONA"

ACT I: SCENE 1

The play begins in an open place in Verona in Shakespeare's day, and immediately we meet the "gentlemen" of the title. Valentine is ready to leave by ship for Milan to take service in the court of the Duke of Milan. He regrets that his friend, Proteus, is staying behind and draws attention to the fact that "Homekeeping youth have ever homely wits," and that affection ought not to interfere with education gained by means of travel.

> COMMENT: It was common sixteenth-century custom, both in England and in Italy, to send young people to the court of some noble person to learn good manners and also to seek suitable marriages. This custom of service to a noble was an important part of education.

Proteus also feels sadness at the departure of his friend, but says that his love for Julia keeps him at home. Valentine makes fun of Proteus, claiming that love has made him effeminate, and that the lover is a fool. "Thou art a votary [devoted worshipper] to fond [foolish] desire." He also details the unhappy symptoms of Proteus' love: the groans with which he receives the scorn of his lady, the sighs which answer the lady's coy looks, and his wearying sleeplessness.

> COMMENT: This account shows that Proteus is the victim of a love that destroys, not ennobles. It also contains the symptoms of the so-called "Petrarchan" or romantic and courtly love which follows a pattern. First, the lover becomes sad and pays no attention to his grooming; then his appetite for food fails; he becomes sleepless, then weak, then lightheaded; finally, he is the complete victim of a paralyzing and excessive love-melancholy.

Valentine departs and Proteus notes that "He after honour hunts, I after love," and says that Julia, his lady, has made him what he is.

> COMMENT: Proteus is here shown as failing in his obligations as a Renaissance gentleman. And, what is worse, he knows it.

At this point, Speed, Valentine's servant, enters. He is a clownish character who puns constantly. He says that he has given a letter to Julia and asks money for his pains.

> COMMENT: This play is full of puns, some rather forced. Remember that the Elizabethans thought the pun an excellent form of wit, and there were at least three different kinds of puns for

various occasions. In this play, the attitude towards puns seems to be "can you top this?"

SUMMARY: This opening scene of exposition is important for the following reasons:

1. It introduces the two major characters of the play, Proteus and Valentine.

2. It establishes the friendship between the young gentleman—an extremely important element throughout the play.

3. It establishes Valentine as an ambitious seeker after honor and a scoffer at love.

4. It shows Proteus paralyzed into inactivity by an excess of love as he dotes on Julia.

5. It raises important questions of education, travel, and experience, as well as the duties of a gentleman.

6. It introduces us to Speed, the clownish servant of Valentine. In his speeches, we discover the principal form of verbal wit which will be employed in the play: a series of puns revolving around a central metaphor.

ACT I: SCENE 2

This scene takes place in the garden of Julia's house in Verona. Julia is talking to Lucetta, her waiting-woman, about her lovers, mentioning their names and having the maid give a brief sketch of them. Apparently, there are three suitors: Sir Eglamour, a fine knight; Sir Mercatio, a wealthy man; and Proteus, whom Lucetta thinks rather foolish.

> **COMMENT:** This incident introduces Julia as a girl with many suitors. Note that the Sir Eglamour of Act I does not seem to be the same character as in Act IV. The single-lined speech which is immediately capped by a similar speech from a different character is a device derived from classical drama and is called *stychomythia.*

Lucetta has brought the letter from Proteus which Speed mentioned in the previous scene. Julia refuses to take it at first, then regrets her action: obviously she is in love, but she will not admit it. She recalls Lucetta, and after a series of punning speeches based on a music metaphor, she takes the letter with a show of anger and tears it across. But once Lucetta has left she crawls around trying to put the pieces back together. The letter seems to be a conventional love letter full of the plaints and complaints we would expect of Proteus.

SUMMARY: This scene serves the following purposes:

1. It introduces Julia as a witty young lady who is obviously in love with Proteus, but who is determined to keep both him and her maid guessing.

2. It introduces the minor character of the maid, Lucetta.

3. It provides dramatic exposition. The device of the catalogue of suitors is used later in *The Merchant of Venice*.

4. The letter, when reassembled, gives further evidence of the nature of Proteus' affection.

ACT I: SCENE 3

This scene takes place a short time later in the house of Antonio, father of Proteus. He is speaking with a friend, Panthino, who is detailing a conversation he has had with Antonio's brother about Proteus. The brother has wondered why Antonio has allowed Proteus to stay home while other young men have been permitted to travel, to seek honor in the wars, and to gain various other educational experiences. Antonio admits that he, too, is upset, and says that he has been trying to think of what to do about Proteus. Panthino then recalls that Valentine is already at the Emperor's court and suggests that, since a mutual friend, Don Alphonso, is about to leave for Milan, it would now be a good time to send Proteus.

> **COMMENT:** This scene discusses at some length the Renaissance theories of the education of a young nobleman (I.iii.4-33). He should learn from books, travel, experience, and the behavior of residents at a great court. Note the apparent error: Valentine is with the *Duke* of Milan, where Proteus later joins him.

Proteus then enters avidly reading a letter from Julia. When his father asks about it, Proteus lies, saying that it is from Valentine. That statement gives Antonio his opportunity to tell his son his plans for his future. As the two older men leave, Proteus speaks of his sorrow in having to leave Julia.

> **COMMENT:** This last speech of Proteus has the tone of Shakespeare's sonnets which are concerned with love and friendship. There seem to be many echoes of the sonnets in this play.

SUMMARY: This scene serves several functions, both for the advancement of the plot, and for establishing intellectual background.

1. It acts as a means of furthering the plot by having Proteus sent to court.

2. It discusses and illustrates Renaissance theories of the education of a young gentleman.

3. It shows Proteus as deficient in education and, even, in some aspects of morality. He lies rather too easily.

4. It shows the control of a parent over his child. Proteus does not dare defy his father. Parental power comes up again in the play with reference to the lady Silvia.

ACT II: SCENE 1

This scene takes place in Milan at the palace of the Duke. Valentine and Speed enter. Speed gives Valentine a glove that the young man has dropped absent-mindedly. He, himself, now, is sighing and groaning for the love of Silvia. Speed scoffs at him by detailing the symptoms of his love which are the same as those he has so often ridiculed in Proteus. The two men then discuss the beauty and virtue of Silvia until Speed says that, as a lover, Valentine cannot possibly be objective.

Silvia herself enters and Valentine offers her the letter she had commanded him to write to a "secret nameless friend" of hers. He protests that he found the letter extremely hard to write, and, in fact, has written it unwillingly. Silvia promptly returns the letter to him since it was written with bad grace, and, therefore, not movingly. Much to Speed's amusement, the lady leaves. The servant, who is not romantically involved with the lady, realizes that Silvia is making Valentine write a love letter to himself.

> **COMMENT:** This incident shows how far Valentine has fallen in love. As usual, Speed makes witty comments and puns. The lady Silvia's flirting with her lover is similar to the action of Julia earlier in the play; indeed, the two affairs are deliberately made parallel.

At the end of the scene, Speed thinks of dinner, but Valentine says that he has already dined—on the sight of his lady!

SUMMARY: This scene indicates how far Valentine's education has progressed.

1. Far from pursuing honor, Valentine has fallen as deeply into love-melancholy as his friend. He is quite blind to the joke that Silvia has played upon him.

2. Speed is now the scoffer at love, but he cannot make his master see reason.

3. Silvia is introduced as a witty, beautiful lady who plays with the lover who is her abject servant.

4. Shakespeare has now set up an almost symmetrical plot with two sets of lovers. (With Launce's entry, we later discover that there are two witty servant-clowns as well.)

ACT II: SCENES 2-3

The first of these scenes takes place in Julia's house in Verona—it is a touching farewell between Proteus and Julia. Both declare their love and

exchange rings and "seal the bargain with a holy kiss," while Proteus takes
Julia's hand.

> **COMMENT:** This scene contains the elements of a valid contract
> to marry at a future date. No words to that effect are spoken, but
> they are implicit. The actions of the couple are the outward signs
> of such a contract. Such an engagement can be broken only by
> mutual consent, or due to the misbehavior of one of the parties.

The next scene takes place in a street in Verona. Launce, the clownish
servant of Proteus, and his dog are introduced. Launce tells the sad tale
of his departure from home and he tries to re-enact the weeping in the
household. He also rebukes his dog for its heartlessness in not joining in
the general grief.

> **COMMENT:** This interlude is meant as a parody of the preceding
> scene. It undercuts the emotions of Julia and Proteus and reduces
> them to the same level as that of Launce and his dog. This device of
> parody is a common one in comedy. Later in his writing career,
> Shakespeare sometimes has the parody precede the relatively serious
> scene.

Panthino enters and tells Launce to embark on the waiting ship. After
more witty puns, Launce and the older man leave.

SUMMARY: Scenes 2-3 should be treated together because of their
function in the play.

1. The scenes are important in advancing the plot. Proteus must leave
Verona.

2. They contrast with each other. The farewell of Proteus and Julia is
parodied by Launce and his dog.

3. The scene between Proteus and Julia shows them as engaged to marry,
which makes Proteus's later unfaithfulness more despicable.

4. The exchange of rings provides a tangible means for future identification, as well as being the symbol of the engagement.

5. The parody shows that Shakespeare does not mean us to take Proteus
too seriously.

6. We are introduced to Launce and his dog. (Launce and Speed are two
of Shakespeare's earliest funny men.)

ACT II: SCENE 4

This scene takes place a short time later in the Duke's palace in Milan.
Silvia, Valentine, Speed, and Thurio enter. Thurio will gain more significance later. He is much older than Valentine and is in love with Silvia,

who is not fond of him; therefore, she speaks kindly to her "servant" Valentine.

> **COMMENT:** This continual use of the word "servant" in Valentine's relationship with Silvia indicates an affair conducted on a courtly basis, following the "rules" of courtly love.

The Duke enters and asks Valentine about Proteus, who proves his friendship by giving a glowing account of Proteus. He is amazed to learn that Proteus has arrived and wonders about the progress of his love affair with Julia. He cannot believe that she has rejected his friend. Proteus and Valentine then greet each other; Silvia, Thurio, and the Duke leave them together. Then Valentine asks about Proteus' love affair with Julia. To Proteus' surprise, he discovers that his friend is now as deeply in love with Silvia as he, himself, is with Julia. It is now the turn of Proteus to be more levelheaded than his friend, for he praises Silvia as "an earthly paragon," not "a heavenly saint." Valentine then identifies Thurio as his rival suitor who is favored by the Duke because of his wealth.

> **COMMENT:** A good sixteenth-century father always thought about his daughter's financial security. The wishes of the girl were not often considered, and the existence of love before marriage was distrusted because it might cool, especially if the couple were poor.

Valentine then confides to his friend that he and Silvia plan to elope and be married without the consent of the Duke. In fact, Valentine has already arranged for a rope ladder so that Silvia can climb down from her window. Valentine asks the help of Proteus who refuses, saying he has other business to attend to. Left alone, Proteus speaks of the way in which he has fallen in love with Silvia at first sight. He then discusses the central conflict of the play—that between love and friendship.

> **COMMENT:** Proteus has obviously fallen into a mad passion that has overwhelmed his reason. He thinks only of how to gratify his lust for Sylvia, and the superior claims of friendship mean nothing to him. It was believed in the Renaissance that friendship held the highest claims of all upon a man. Friendship between men and women was imperfect because physical love entered into it, but friendship between men of equal station was perfect because it existed only on a spiritual level.

SUMMARY: This scene is important because of the added complications it introduces.

1. We meet Sir Thurio, the Duke's candidate for Silvia's hand.

2. We learn of Valentine's projected elopement.

3. We discover that Proteus is so deeply in love with Silvia that he is willing to abandon friendship for an excessive and sudden love.

ACT II: SCENES 5-6

The first of these scenes takes place in a street of Milan. Launce and Speed discourse wittily with each other on the progress of the love affairs of their respective masters.

> **COMMENT:** This brief comic interlude is sandwiched between two soliloquies of Proteus and serves to make fun of the vagaries of love. At the same time, it gives the audience time to recover from the shock of Proteus' ignoble behavior.

The next scene takes place inside the Duke's palace and we find Proteus still wrestling with his love problem. He praises Silvia as superior to Julia in every way, and he fully understands that, in yielding to this passion, he will be doubly disloyal—both to Julia and to Valentine. Nevertheless, he decides to choose passionate love over friendship and says that he will tell the Duke of Valentine's plans.

SUMMARY: These scenes are important for their contrast, and the soliloquy of Proteus initiates much of the future action of the play.

1. Launce and Speed serve as comic relief between Proteus' two soliloquies.

2. Proteus decides to betray his friendship and to tell the Duke of Valentine's plans.

3. The character of Proteus is revealed as one that is rather unstable and given to sudden passions and changes of mind. His passion now controls his reason—a dangerous and uncontrolled condition.

ACT II: SCENE 6

This scene takes place in Julia's house in Verona. Julia tells Lucetta that she is thinking of following her beloved Proteus to Milan. Since it would be unseemly for a young lady to travel alone, Julia wishes to go disguised as a page.

> **COMMENT:** These "trouser parts" and disguises for girls were common in Italian comedy. Further, since all women's parts were played by young boys in the Elizabethan theatre, the disguises were easily acceptable. Remember, as a dramatic convention, all disguises were considered impenetrable.

Julia then speaks glowingly of the loyalty of her Proteus, while Lucetta skeptically hopes that such a trust is justified.

COMMENT AND SUMMARY: The position of this tender scene forms an ironic contrast to the disloyalty of Proteus. The short scene also advances the plot by having Julia disguise herself as a boy in order to follow Proteus.

ACT III: SCENE 1

This scene takes place shortly after Proteus' soliloquies and within the Duke's palace in Milan. At first, the Duke, Proteus, and Thurio are present, but Thurio is sent away. Proteus speaks rather pompously about "the law of friendship" which would forbid him to tell what he is about to tell the Duke. He proceeds rather smugly to ingratiate himself by announcing that the claims of duty to the Duke are higher than those of friendship. Then, on the request of the Duke he reveals Valentine's plans to elope with Silvia. When Valentine enters, the Duke plays cat-and-mouse with him, forcing him to praise Thurio for virtues which his rival does not possess.

The Duke then proceeds to tell Valentine that he has decided to disinherit the disobedient Silvia and take a wife himself. Under this pretext he asks Valentine for assistance in his wooing and gradually coerces the unfortunate young man to reveal his own plot to elope with Silvia. The rope ladder, together with a love poem, is found in Valentine's possession so the Duke, in anger, banishes him from the court. Valentine is grief-stricken and, like Romeo, thinks seriously of suicide. He is about to kill himself when Launce and Proteus enter. After some byplay, Proteus laments Valentine's situation and tells his friend that the Duke has had Silvia imprisoned. He then recommends that Valentine depart from Milan and offers to escort him to the gate.

COMMENT: The honesty of Valentine is shown most brightly in opposition to the treacherous hypocrisy of Proteus. As an extenuating circumstance one must, however, recall that Proteus' reason is so overcome by his passion that he is not fully responsible for his actions.

Launce is left alone on the stage; we find that he is in love also. He laments his state and catalogues the advantages of his mistress—a tough, strong milkmaid. Once again, Shakespeare has us laugh at the follies of all levels of lovers. Speed enters and they discuss Launce's lady whose virtues parody almost all of those expected in women. Then, after having wasted his time, Speed tells Launce that his master wants him to hurry after him.

SUMMARY: This very long scene has several important functions in advancing the plot and revealing character.

1. It shows Proteus revealing Valentine's plot to the Duke.

2. It presents Proteus in a most unflattering light because he is smug, pompous, disloyal; he lies to his friend; and he violates the codes of both love and friendship.

3. It exposes Valentine as a true lover, but a rather inexperienced plotter, because he allows himself to be outmaneuvered by the Duke. His fidelity is indicated by his contemplation of suicide.

4. It reveals the character of the Duke as a father who wants complete control over his daughter.

5. It illustrates Silvia's fidelity to Valentine, even at the risk of imprisonment.

6. It parodies the entire business of love-making in the repetition of the *catalogue scene* of II.iv in a different setting with Launce and Speed as the principals.

ACT III: SCENE 2

This scene takes place in the Duke's palace in Milan shortly after the banishment of Valentine. Thurio complains that Silvia has despised him utterly since Valentine's banishment, but the Duke, and later, Proteus, agree that her grief will eventually lessen. Proteus first suggests slandering Valentine. Then he suggests that Thurio attempt to gain Silvia's heart by means of the code of courtly wooing, with letters, poems, and music, in particular. Thurio says he will try music and a poem this very evening.

SUMMARY: This scene ties up the events of Act III and contrasts the loyalty of Silvia with the disloyalty of Proteus who is about to be disloyal for the third time when he plots against the Duke and Thurio.

ACT IV: SCENE 1

This scene takes place in a forest on the frontiers of Mantua. Valentine and Speed are captured by a band of outlaws who ask for money, to which Valentine replies that he has no more than the clothes he wears. After some questioning, Valentine says that he is on his way to Verona after having killed a man in Milan in a fair fight.

> **COMMENT:** The only reason for this lie seems to be a desire to impress the outlaws of the forest.

On hearing that Valentine is "A linguist and a man of such perfection," the outlaws invite him to become their leader, telling him that some of them are gentlemen. They claim that their crimes were minor; however, they offer the young man little alternative to acceptance. Valentine, stipulating that the outlaws attack no defenseless women or poor travelers, becomes the leader of the outlaw band.

> **COMMENT AND SUMMARY:** Perhaps the outlaws pick Valentine as a leader because they can recognize true nobility and loyalty. The interlude in the wood serves largely to project a grand meeting in the forest later.

ACT IV: SCENE 2

This scene takes place a short time later in Milan, outside the Duke's palace and under the window of Silvia's chamber. Proteus begins with an account of the extent of his disloyalty, first to Valentine, and now to Thurio.

Clearly, Silvia remains faithful to Valentine and she upbraids Proteus for his disloyalty to Julia. But nothing seems to lessen his passion for Silvia; he has forgotten all sense of duty. Thurio arrives with musicians to entertain Silvia.

> **COMMENT:** Music, "the food of love" was supposed to be very powerful in arousing love in the bosom of a lady. Serenading the lady from beneath her window was, and is, considered a high compliment.

In the distance, Julia appears in disguise, accompanied by the Host of the inn who is taking her to Proteus. She chances on this musical scene, from which she draws the obvious conclusion. After the musicians sing the famous "Who is Silvia," they depart with Thurio, and Silvia chides Proteus for infidelity to Julia. To Julia's sorrow, she hears Proteus lie in announcing that she is dead. Silvia then urges on Proteus the claims of friendship with Valentine, but the young man claims that his friend is also dead. Silvia then promises Proteus a portrait which, as an imitation of her, is a falsehood, and, therefore, well suited to a false man.

COMMENT AND SUMMARY: This idea of the imitation of life as a form of falsehood comes from Plato. The scene is concerned with the conflict of loyalties. The loyalty of Silvia, and also that of the hidden Julia, both contrast with the falsehood of Proteus.

ACT IV: SCENE 3

This scene also takes place below Silvia's window, a short time later. Silvia enlists the help of Sir Eglamour in escaping from Milan. She wishes to go to Mantua to be with Valentine. Silvia conveys to us the sad story of Sir Eglamour and we find that here we have a true servant of love, a man who is so loyal to the memory of his dead lady that he has sworn eternal chastity. He is a completely worthy escort for the loyal Silvia. For him service to love, rather than the possession of the beloved, is important. Silvia makes arrangements to meet Eglamour at Friar Patrick's cell the coming evening.

SUMMARY: This scene shows us other aspects of loyalty in love and it also helps to advance the action.

1. Sir Eglamour (not the suitor mentioned in Act I) adds another aspect of love—service as a courtly ideal. He helps ladies in distress for the sake of his own dead lady.

2. Silvia will do anything in order to remain loyal to Valentine and to avoid marriage to Thurio.

3. These two characters present an implied contrast to Proteus.

ACT IV: SCENE 4

This scene takes place under Silvia's window like the two preceding scenes. Launce enters to tell us that he had obeyed his master Proteus and had given his dog to Silvia. Then he re-enacts all the confusion caused by the lowbred little beast. At this point, Proteus, accompanied by Julia disguised as a page called Sebastian, comes in. After some discussion with Launce, the story comes out: Launce had been ordered to take a dog to Silvia as a gift from Proteus. Unfortunately Launce lost the first dog and offered her, instead, his little mongrel. With rage, Proteus sends Launce away to find the lost dog, and he then sends Julia to Silvia to give to her the ring that Julia had earlier given to him. After expressions of love and sorrow, Julia prepares to carry out Proteus' command.

> **COMMENT:** This convention of a disguised page being sent to woo for her master will be used also in *Twelfth Night*. It is an indication of Julia's love and loyalty that she will work against her own best interests in this regard.

Silvia then keeps her part of the bargain, giving Julia a picture of herself to take to Proteus; at the same time, she upbraids him for disloyalty to his betrothed, Julia. Silvia refuses to read Proteus' letter and is shocked again by Proteus' disloyalty when she recognizes the ring that Julia has brought with her. Julia then tells Silvia of her own pathetic state: loving, but not loved. Silvia is greatly affected by this recital. After Silvia's departure Julia eagerly compares herself with the picture, believing that she, herself, is superior in beauty.

SUMMARY: This scene is important for its revelation of character.

1. It begins with the comic relief of Launce and his dog.

2. It shows how much Proteus dotes on Silvia: he has bought her a little dog, and he sends Julia's ring to her as a love token.

3. It reveals the loyalty and love of Julia who fulfills the commands of her unworthy lover.

4. It illustrates the loyalty and honesty of Silvia. She shows pity for the neglected Julia and sends messages to Proteus which show how much she despises him for his actions.

5. It also emphasizes the understandable feelings of jealousy in Julia who has been supplanted by someone no more beautiful than herself. Julia is a woman with the conventional Elizabethan characteristics: yellow hair, gray eyes, and high forehead.

ACT V: SCENES 1-2

The first scene takes place outside an abbey in Milan the same evening. Eglamour is joined by Silvia and the two depart for the forest. This is Eglamour's last appearance in the play.

The second scene takes place in the Duke's palace in Milan. Thurio asks Proteus, who is accompanied by his page (the disguised Julia), about the progress of his suit to Silvia. The scene then resolves itself in a three-way conversation in which Julia's asides reduce the remarks of both Thurio and Proteus to their comic essentials. In the midst of the discussion, the Duke reveals that Silvia has disappeared and he concludes that she must have gone to look for Valentine. The Duke announces his departure to find his daughter. Thurio says he will join him to be revenged on Eglamour; Proteus says he will go for love of Silvia; and Julia says that she will go in order to cross Proteus' love for Silvia.

SUMMARY: These two scenes really act as a bridge to keep various parts of the plot moving. Everyone is obviously going to meet in the forest and we can anticipate a grand confrontation scene soon.

ACT V: SCENES 3-4

This extremely short scene is placed in the forest on the frontiers of Mantua. Silvia has been captured by the outlaws who plan to take her to their leader, Valentine.

The next scene takes place in another part of the same forest. Valentine enters and indulges himself in a soliloquy of love-melancholy. When he hears noises in the forest, he hides to observe what is going on. Proteus, Silvia, and Julia then enter, the young man having just rescued Silvia from the outlaws. Much to the horror of the hidden Valentine, he asks for her love, and when Silvia continues to withstand him despite all his arguments, he speaks the last and ultimate words of his disloyalty to Valentine: "In love/Who respects friend?" Silvia says that Proteus alone is such a man. Proteus precipitously tries to force himself upon her in an act of rape.

> **COMMENT:**   This attempt represents the depth of Proteus' degradation, as he is maddened by lust rather than love. Lust makes him insensible to all the dictates of goodness and virtue.

Valentine leaps from his hiding place and reviles Proteus for his actions. But, above all, he regrets the sundering of a friendship. Proteus immediately repents. He is brought to his senses and asks forgiveness.

> **COMMENT:**   This sudden repentance seems more unconvincing to us than it would have to the Elizabethans. It was believed then that various attitudes and personality traits, and even behavior, were the result of an imbalance in the four bodily fluids. One attitude could consequently be replaced by its opposite by means of a sudden shock. We must accept Proteus' repentance in this spirit.

Valentine is overcome by an excess of friendliness and forgives Proteus in an astonishing line: "All that was mine in Silvia I give thee." Julia swoons.

> **COMMENT:**   Valentine's action seems inexplicable. In effect, it signifies tremendous magnanimity (generosity) on Valentine's part. He is performing the greatest possible act of friendship, while Proteus, if totally repentant would, or rather should, refuse the offer

As it is he says nothing, because his attentions are engaged with his swooning page.

On recovering her senses, Julia tells Proteus that she had forgotten to deliver his ring to Silvia. Proteus looks at it and sees that it is actually the ring that he, himself, had given to Julia. After some quibbling about how the ring came to be in "Sebastian's" possession, Julia reveals her identity and begs to be absolved from any immodesty, since it is a lesser blot for a woman to change her clothes than for a man to change his mind.

> **COMMENT:** It is impossible to determine what Shakespeare intended by the confusion of the rings except to use it for the revelation of Julia's identity. At this point, Julia administers a mild rebuke to Proteus, which hurts him.

Proteus looks at Julia with new eyes and begins to wonder what he had seen in Sylvia. The two friends now embrace and of course Proteus has, by his actions, refused Valentine's offer of Silvia.

The Duke and Thurio, having been captured by the outlaws, are brought in. Valentine restrains his men, but Thurio calls for Silvia. Valentine immediately threatens him with death if he should even mention her name, and the cowardly knight subsides, mumbling that he does not want to endanger his body for a girl who does not love him. At these words, the Duke is enraged. He sees Thurio for the "degenerate and base" man that he is and praises Valentine as "a gentleman and well derived."

> **COMMENT:** This distinction between nobility of birth and nobility of action was a common one in the Renaissance. It was generally held that all nobility must be confirmed by noble and virtuous action; Thurio, though of higher birth than Valentine, had failed to confirm his superiority by action.

Now that Valentine is considered noble, he is worthy of Silvia, and the Duke offers her to him. After thanking the Duke, Valentine makes a last request that again reveals his nobility. He asks amnesty for his outlaw band, claiming that they are now reformed characters. The Duke grants pardons to them as asked. As yet, the Duke does not know the identity of Julia, and Valentine teasingly promises to tell the Duke the whole story on the way back to Milan. The play ends on a note of reconciliation, with the promise of a double wedding.

SUMMARY: This last scene constitutes the unraveling of all the complications of the play.

1. Everyone meets in the forest for a confrontation scene.

2. Proteus goes to the utmost depths of disloyalty in trying to force himself upon Silvia.

3. The arrival of Valentine makes Proteus repent, while Valentine's

magnanimous offer of Silvia signifies perfect forgiveness on the part of the wronged friend.

4. The page Sebastian is revealed as Julia, and she, too, forgives Proteus after a mild rebuke.

5. Sir Thurio is revealed as a coward.

6. The Duke's eyes are opened; he sees the innate nobility of Valentine and finds him worthy of marriage to Silvia.

7. Valentine asks amnesty for his outlaw friends, a request that the Duke is glad to grant.

8. All members of the group are reconciled; the play ends with the prospect of a double marriage ceremony.

CHARACTER ANALYSES: "THE TWO GENTLEMEN OF VERONA"

PROTEUS: He is truly the central character of the play (protagonist) which is one of the reasons that the play has never been popular. He is an unsympathetic young man because of his disloyalty and we find it difficult to accept him as a hero. There are many questions about him that remain unanswered. What, for instance, is his initial feeling for Julia? It would seem that he is in love with her in the romantic, courtly sense, and he fulfills the customary functions of such a lover. But his love is so excessive that it can be called "dotage," and it has plunged him into a state of paralyzing inactivity rather than ennobling him. When he falls in love with Silvia suddenly we are shocked, but he is a young man of extremes, and when he is under the control of a governing passion he is almost powerless to fight it. He wallows in affection for Julia, but his affection for Silvia is lustful, as proved in his final, wanton attempt to rape her. Sexual passion has completely numbed his reason. He does not care even for friendship, an attitude which leads him to the betrayal of Valentine and his attempt on Silvia. Nevertheless, as soon as he is made to see the folly and the horror of his ways, he repents.

VALENTINE: He is a character of more nobility and more consistency than Proteus. He has his own view of love. Like Proteus, he begins by an excess of affection, but he seems to have more vitality than Proteus, and he thinks of his career as well. He wishes to be the epitome of the Renaissance gentleman at the beginning of the play, and he conscientiously sets out to educate himself. He also seems to possess some natural authority, because the outlaws welcome him as a leader. Moreover, he is a generous, forgiving young man who goes so far as to offer his repentant friend the person he loves best, Silvia. He is completely loyal to the claims of friendship and, in that regard, is a foil to Proteus. Finally, he proves himself noble by his deeds rather than by his birth, and supports all who have helped him, even the outlaws, for whom he manages to obtain pardons.

JULIA: She is a well-drawn figure and is the embodiment of femininity, fidelity, and love. She will dare anything to go to her beloved. Nevertheless, when he is near her at the beginning of the play, she is capable of making fun of both him and his letters. She is utterly faithful to Proteus, despite his indifference towards her, and she even undertakes to woo Silvia for him—since that is what he appears to want. Finally, her disguise as a page is penetrated by means of a confusion of rings. Her fidelity is rewarded and she forgives Proteus. If one thinks that the young man is unworthy of her, one should remember that he has probably learned a lesson.

SILVIA: She is a fairly well-delineated figure, but we see only one aspect of her—her loyalty. She possesses a considerable amount of initiative and upbraids the lovers she does not want. On occasion, she can be disobedient to her father where her heart is concerned and she continually chastizes Proteus for his disloyalty. She, like Julia, is careful of her reputation, but her solution of her romance is different. Rather than dress as a boy, she finds Sir Eglamour to take her into the forest. She is totally virtuous and seems to play the part of conscience in the play.

SIR EGLAMOUR: He is a minor character, a votary of love who has sworn perpetual chastity on the grave of his dead lady. He gives his life to love's service, which he prefers to the actual possession of a lady. He is the embodiment of everlasting loyalty and a latter-day knight who helps maidens in distress.

SIR THURIO: He is the Duke's candidate for Silvia's hand, but he seems to possess little more than lands. He is rather a blusterer, and is finally exposed as a coward.

THE DUKE OF MILAN: He is the patron of Valentine and Proteus. He is, primarily, a stock character—the hostile father who wishes his daughter to marry only whom he wants, and he expects complete obedience. He is not concerned with such matters as love before marriage, but prefers to have his daughter well provided for where money is concerned. He is enlightened in the forest where he is shown the cowardice of Thurio and the nobility of Valentine. He then admits his error and consents to the match between Valentine and Silvia.

LUCETTA: She is a minor character, the maid to Julia, but is one of the first of a long line of witty and resourceful serving wenches. She understands the course of her mistress's love affair very well indeed, and it is she who obtains the disguise for Julia.

LAUNCE AND SPEED: These two characters should be dealt with together because they complement each other. Launce is the servant of Proteus and is a dull-witted country boy, accompanied by his dog. He continually misunderstands, not fully understanding what is meant because his vocabulary is based on the heard, rather than the written, word. He is at his best in parody. He is given the task of burlesquing Proteus' leave-taking of Julia and also that of parodying the various aspects of courtly love: praise of the beloved, and the giving of gifts to a lady. He acts as a foil to Speed, the servant of Valentine, who, as his name implies, has a quicker mind. He is capable of carrying on a verbal joke for a considerable time and can hunt a metaphor through a thicket of wit. He is a rogue, but one with great cleverness. These servants are the first of a long line of Shakespearean clowns.

ANTONIO AND PANTHINO: These are characters who are barely touched upon. Antonio, the father of Proteus, and his friend, Panthino, appear only in one scene. The latter, however, has some importance as a mouthpiece for some of the most prevalent Renaissance attitudes towards the education of young gentlemen.

ESSAY QUESTIONS FOR REVIEW: "THE TWO GENTLEMEN OF VERONA"

1. How many different attitudes towards love can you find in this play?

There are six different attitudes towards love in this play. The *first* is that held originally by Proteus, and, later, by his friend, Valentine. This is a romantic attitude in which the lover sighs, forgets to eat, is unable to sleep, neglects his personal appearance, and in general, is reduced to paralyzed inactivity. In some respects such lovers are in love with the state of being in love, rather than loving the alleged object of their affections.

The *second* attitude is held by both Julia and Silvia. These ladies are passionately in love with their men and they are also completely faithful to them. But they do not luxuriate in their passion. Julia follows Proteus to court in order to be near him, while Silvia thinks nothing of fleeing from Milan in order to avoid a disagreeable marriage.

The *third* attitude is a mildly cynical one that is held by Lucetta, Julia's maid, and also Valentine, at the beginning. Lucetta laughs at her mistress's suitors, but, at the same time, she helps Julia disguise herself in order to follow Proteus. At first, Valentine laughs at Proteus, the slave of love, but almost as a kind of punishment he later falls even more deeply in love with Sylvia.

The *fourth* attitude is that of the Duke of Milan, who seems to believe that he can dictate love to his daughter; therefore, he attempts to force Silvia into an unwanted match with Sir Thurio, the knight. Ironically, Sir Thurio adopts all the outward trappings of a romantic passion, with poems to the beauty of his mistress, and musicians to sing beneath her window. But he is a coward and is eventually found out.

The *fifth* attitude is that held by Sir Eglamour, and it is in some ways a composite of some of the other views. Since the death of his lady, Sir Eglamour has sworn perpetual chastity and fidelity to her memory. As a result, he is a knightly votary of love who aids maidens in distress.

To him, service to the idea of love is more important than possession of a beloved lady.

The *sixth* attitude towards love may be described as almost a momentary aberration arising from the first one—that of excessive romantic passion. This is held by Proteus who falls in love (as he thinks) with Silvia at first sight, and later gives in to his lust and attempts to rape her in order to possess her. We should not, however, be too hard on Proteus, because he repents as soon as his friend shows him his error.

2. What are the principal dramatic devices used in this play?

This play is important because it uses effectively many dramatic devices that reappear in other comedies. There are five in particular. First, we have the contrasting pairs of lovers who appear in most of the earlier and later comedies. Second, there is the girl disguised as a page who appears in *As You Like It* and *Twelfth Night*. Note too that Julia, like Viola in *Twelfth Night*, is sent by her lover to carry messages of love to her rival, and, in her fidelity, she complies. Third, we have a pair of clowns who are the predecessors of many who enliven proceedings in such plays as *Much Ado About Nothing* and *The Merchant of Venice*. Fourth, we have, in addition, the debates on love and friendship which bear considerable resemblance to the kind of situation described in Shakespeare's sonnets. Fifth, we have the young romantic lovers who are in love with love, like Orlando in *As You Like It* and Orsino in *Twelfth Night*. *The Two Gentlemen* is a compendium of Shakespearean dramatic devices.

3. What is the code of friendship implied in this play?

The code of friendship in this play is basically that of Aristotle in his *Nichomachean Ethics*, Books VIII-IX. Here, the philosopher praises friendship between equals in which young men share all their secrets and engage themselves to be loyal to each other in all things, and, if necessary, to help each other, most notably in war, but also in love. By attempting to steal Silvia away from Valentine, Proteus has sinned against friendship, and he compounds the fault by revealing the secret of his friend's proposed elopement to the Duke. Finally, by attempting to rape Silvia, he shows himself to be without shame and as having completely violated the code. By contrast, Valentine is totally forgiving, like a perfect friend, when he offers Silvia, his most prized possession, to his friend. This last action not only signifies the forgiveness of Valentine, but also the fact that the friendship of men should be superior to the love of a woman. In refusing the offer, Proteus reveals his own repentance.

'LOVE'S LABOUR'S LOST'

THE PLAY: *Love's Labour's Lost* in many ways has become dated far more than any other Shakespearean production. Chiefly, we find that there are many topical references to people actually alive at the time whose portraits would have been recognized by members of the original audience. We, however, have lost the key to the identities of these persons; thus, a substantial reservoir of fun has disappeared for us. Further, our sense of humor is different in that we do not appreciate jokes about the style of writers whom none of us read today. And, of course, we often consider puns to be a weak form of humor, whereas the Elizabethans did not. But, even if we do not understand all the finer points of Shakespeare's jokes, we can still understand very well the basic situation in which four unwilling young men give up love for study and then fall in love with four merry ladies. Love is the theme of the play, and the truest study is shown to be that which is based on a knowledge and understanding of love in its finest sense. The subplot shows us very clearly that physical love is considered inferior to an affection of the mind and the passions. Finally, as the title indicates, the play ends in sorrow, parting, and death. *Love's Labour's Lost*—but only for the time being.

SOURCE AND TEXT: This play is possibly wholly of Shakespeare's invention, but there may be references to contemporary historical events, which, however, do not help us in assigning a definite date to the play. The date, 1593-94, is the one usually accepted, chiefly because the frequent use of rhyme, doggerel, puns, and the general style of the blank verse indicate it is an early play. The emphasis on rhetorical and linguistic comedy also leads us to conclude that it was written for a courtly and cultivated audience rather than for the motley crowd at the Globe.

Love's Labour's Lost was first published in 1598 in a badly printed quarto edition and was reprinted in 1607. It was the first of the early Shakespearean comedies to be published, and was reprinted in the First Folio, 1623, in a text that seems to have followed that of the 1598 quarto. It is also possible that the play contains revisions which were not clarified. For instance, the speech identifications are not consistent in IV.ii, and in two other scenes (IV.iii.296-307 and V.ii.827-832) we have lines that have their sense repeated in an expanded form.

THE PLOT: Ferdinand, King of Navarre, and his friends, Longaville, Dumain, and Biron, have decided to retire from the world—particularly from the society of ladies—for three years in order to study and to seek fame and glory. As the play opens, the four young men are in the process of signing the oath to fast, to sleep very little, and generally to weaken the flesh in the service of the mind. The King and the first two gentlemen sign readily, but Biron is reluctant. He protests against the harshness of the oath and asks the purpose of study, commenting rather cynically that study blinds both the eyes and the mind. Then he reminds the King that he will have to allow a group of ladies within his court since the

Princess of France and her ladies are on their way on a diplomatic mission from the French king. The King says that, in this case, the oath must be dispensed with, but Biron insists upon the observance of both the spirit and the letter of the oath, to which he then, with a flourish, subscribes his name.

At this moment, the Constable, Anthony Dull, drags in a rustic named Costard who has been caught with the dairymaid, Jaquenetta. She is a servant essential to the court, and is the only woman permitted to remain. Dull brings with him a letter setting out the charges against Costard from Don Adriano de Armado, a pedantic Spaniard whose vocabulary is composed of "fire-new words" and whose rhetoric is a remarkable achievement. Dull spends a great deal of time misusing words, and Costard makes clownish remarks. The King sends Costard to Armado who must have the clown fast as punishment for his designs on Jaquenetta. We then meet the pretentious Armado with his page, Moth, and the inarticulate and rather saucy Jaquenetta.

The Princess of France arrives with her ladies: Rosaline, a dark-haired, dark-eyed beauty; Katharine, a red-gold lady; and Maria. Within a few minutes, we find out that each of the ladies is in love with one of the gentlemen of the court of Navarre: Rosaline is in love with Biron, Katharine with Dumain, and Maria with Longaville. The King and his gentlemen appear and the Princess begins to bargain for the rights of her father in Aquitaine. But, since some essential documents have not yet arrived, the ladies must stay in the vicinity (though not in the court itself) until the next day. In the course of conversation the young people pair off.

Armado and Moth then appear. After a witty exchange, Armado gives Costard, the rustic, a love letter to deliver to Jaquenetta. The pedant has fallen desperately in love with the illiterate girl. Biron then enters and gives Costard a letter to be delivered to Rosaline. For a moment, Biron is alone and we learn that he is hopelessly, but rather unwillingly, in love with Rosaline, whose beauty is not of the conventional type.

The Princess and her retinue are hunting in the park when Costard arrives with the letter for Rosaline which, at the request of the Princess, is read to the assembled company. Unfortunately, Costard has confused the letters and given them to the wrong people. As a result, Rosaline gets the rhetorical flourishes of Don Armado, while Biron's letter has been delivered to Jaquenetta who, being illiterate, has taken it to Holofernes, the pedant, and his admiring friend, Sir Nathaniel, the Curate, to have it read to her. When these two worthy scholars realize what has happened they send the dairymaid to the King to report the misconduct of Biron.

In the meantime, Biron wanders in the woods lamenting his love. He hides himself when the King approaches and is amazed to see his master pull out a piece of paper and then declaim a love poem in praise of the Princess. No sooner has the King finished and hidden himself than

Longaville enters to sing the praises of Maria. Longaville then conceals himself to avoid encountering Dumain who promptly voices a poem in praise of Katharine. Immediately, Longaville reveals himself to castigate Dumain for oath-breaking, but the King steps out and rebukes both of them. Biron leaves his hiding place and upbraids them all. His triumph is short-lived, because Costard and Jaquenetta arrive with Biron's incriminating letter to Rosaline. All the young men now admit that they are in love, and Biron attempts an argument which will prove that, in denying themselves the sight of women's eyes, the students are, in effect, depriving themselves of the truest knowledge there is.

They all then agree to lay siege to the hearts of their ladies, deciding, for no apparent reason, to disguise themselves as Muscovites. When the ladies get wind of the plan they exchange favors and mask themselves so that each man woos the wrong lady. Disappointed, the gentlemen depart and reappear in their own clothing. Immediately, the French ladies mock them by joking about the way the "Muscovites" had wooed them. The suitors realize that they have been tricked. Holofernes, Sir Nathaniel, Moth, Dull, and Costard appear, prepared to perform the pageant of the Nine Worthies for the delight of both courts. Boyet, a visiting French Lord, and Biron make great fun of the performance, and just as the entertainment is at its height, Mercade, another French Lord, brings word that the King of France, the Princess's father, is dead.

This sudden intrusion of sadness forces everyone into action. The Princess announces that she will go home immediately, and all the young men promptly declare their love to their ladies. The Princess is unwilling to give her consent without considerable thought, so she sends the King to do a year of penance in a hermitage in order that he, too, may be certain of his love. At the end of a year, she promises to marry him— if he does not change his mind. Maria and Katharine also give their lovers a year of penance, but Rosaline inflicts the hardest punishment of all. She tells Biron to spend a year in a hospital, jesting in an attempt to cheer the sick. His most difficult term of trial is nonetheless warranted, because he had been the most cynical of all about the oath, and also about love itself. Armado then announces that he has promised to farm the land for three years in order to gain Jaquenetta. And so the play ends with promises of marriage, but without the complete fulfillment of the desires of the young gentlemen.

DETAILED SUMMARY OF "LOVE'S LABOUR'S LOST"

ACT I: SCENE 1

The play opens in the park of Ferdinand, King of Navarre, in the late sixteenth century. The King exhorts his companions, Biron, Longaville, and Dumain to seek fame and honor. In order to do so, the gentlemen of the court should all join together to make Navarre "a little Academe," which will aim to make an art of living.

> **COMMENT:** The search for a reputation that would live after one's death was a common Renaissance preoccupation. The art of living which the lords wish to practice is probably a reference to the Stoic philosophy which held that a wise man should be free from passion and be completely under the control of his reason. The Stoic practiced indifference to both pleasure and pain. The idea of the academy might also have come from the French and Italian academies.

The King then asks the three gentlemen to sign an agreement to stay with him for three years, during which they will follow a program of moral and intellectual development. Longaville signs first, noting that the mind is better fed the more the body is neglected. Dumain agrees and follows suit, saying that he will give up the world to develop philosophically. The third gentleman, Biron, is a trifle reluctant, and, though expressing his delight in study, he takes exception to the rules that none of them is to see a lady, that they must fast once a week, that they must always curb their appetites for food, and, lastly, that they must sleep no more than three hours a night. These, he complains realistically, are rules too hard to keep. Biron then attempts a definition of the end of study and claims that study, in effect, destroys the wits and blinds the mind (and the eyes) of man. After this attack on the ideal of the Academe, the King tells Biron that he may stay elsewhere, but, to everyone's surprise, Biron says that he will sign the agreement.

Biron then proceeds to read its terms aloud, beginning with the first article: that no woman shall come within a mile of the court. The next item states that no man should talk with a woman for three years on penalty of public shame. But, with a certain glee, Biron reminds the King that the French King's daughter is on her way to visit Navarre to discuss the cession of Aquitaine to her father. The King of Navarre has ostensibly forgotten this proposed visit, and says that, obviously, the court must temporarily dispense with the oath. Biron, however, insists on the observance of both the spirit and the letter of the agreement and then signs his name. As he does so, he asks if there is to be any recreation for the courtly company. The King says that amusement will be found in "a refined traveller of Spain" called Don Armado, who will relate the bold doings of Spanish knights in his inimitable English which, as Biron notes, is full of newfangled words. Both Armado and Costard, a country bumpkin, are to provide sport for the Lords.

> **COMMENT:** Biron's comment on Armado's "fire-new words" leads to the principal form of comic device in this play, comedy based on the use and misuse of language. The name Costard also processes comic possibilities, because it meant a large apple, and was also used as a slang term for the head.

At this point, Dull, a constable whose name suits him well, appears with a letter from Don Armado, which states that Costard has been caught with the dairymaid Jaquenetta who, as an essential servant, is the only woman at the court. Within a few moments, we see that Dull habitually tries to use long and very unusual words, but he always gets them wrong. Costard, the rustic clown, also tries to use inflated language and constructions in matters too minor for such ornamentation. But these two are put in the shade once Don Armado's letter is read out. It is a tremendously pompous piece of writing, following a classical manner of speech and also presenting the accusation in a correct, but affected, legal form.

> **COMMENT:** Don Armado seems to have been created to satirize pedantry, or false learning. Some critics have seen in him the personality of the Cambridge scholar, Gabriel Harvey, but the evidence is scanty and the identification cannot be certain. Dull is a first draft of some of Shakespeare's later police constables, like Verges and Dogberry in *Much Ado About Nothing*.

Amado's letter requests, at length, that Costard be punished. The rustic quibbles about the various words which are used to describe Jaquenetta. But, by the end of the scene, he is forced to admit the truth of the charges.

SUMMARY: This important expository scene serves several purposes:

1. It tells us the terms of the agreement and describes the planned academy.

2. It introduces the sceptical and witty Biron who anticipates realistically that one cannot bury the passions entirely.

3. It contrasts him with the King, Longaville, and Dumain, who believe idealistically that study can be the end of life.

4. It introduces Costard the rustic and Dull the constable, indicating that their comic value is to be found in their misuse of language.

5. It brings Don Armado in by proxy and shows him to be a man fascinated by words and the complexities of their arrangement, Armado might possibly be a satire of a topical figure of Shakespeare's day.

6. It foreshadows the breaking of the vow by introducing the subject of the visit of the French Princess and her coterie.

ACT I: SCENE 2

This scene also takes place in the King's park, some distance away, where we meet Don Adriano de Armado in person with his page, Moth. The entire scene is concerned with the comedy of language and logic and we have a great deal of *stychomythia* (alternation of single-line speeches), a device used in Greek drama.

> **COMMENT:** Some critics see Moth as a portrait of Thomas Nashe,

the novelist, pamphlet writer, and journalist from Cambridge University. Nashe was involved in a very witty and bitter pamphlet war with Gabriel Harvey, the Cambridge classicist. This scene may, therefore, be extremely topical, but we have lost the key to most of the references.

After extensive verbal fencing, Armado admits that he is in love with Jaquenetta, the dairymaid. At this point, Dull and Costard appear with the girl herself. They relay the King's message that Armado must keep Costard under his control and make him fast three times a week to tame his flesh. Armado then addresses Jacquenetta, who is overwhelmed with the attention of such a "noble" man and answers only in absurd, slightly saucy, little clichés. Costard is taken into custody by Moth. When he is left alone, Armado launches into a prose *soliloquy* (a speaking of one's thoughts directly to the audience) concerning his love for Jaquenetta. He becomes extremely pompous and complex in his speech and describes his battle with love as a duel.

SUMMARY: This scene helps underline the ridiculous nature of Don Armado's pretensions. Jaquenetta is a simple, illiterate rustic, and Armado's passion for her is predominantly physical. The man who pretends to be learned and to cultivate the mind is shown to be merely a hypocritical pedant, a man of false learning, who is susceptible to fleshly pleasures.

ACT II: SCENE 1

The Princess of France and her ladies, Rosaline, Maria, and Katharine, then appear in the King's park, accompanied by Boyet, a French lord. He commences by giving the Princess advice on the conduct of her embassy, suggesting that she make use of her beauty to influence the King to arrange the most favorable terms for France. The Princess recalls the nature of the King's oath, so she sends Boyet to speak with him. Then she asks one of her own lords the names of the gentlemen who have taken the vow to study with the King. To her surprise, her own three ladies know the gentlemen concerned, and, from their individual comments on specific lords, she begins to suspect that all three of them are in love. Maria first gives an account of Longaville who, she says, is a perfect gentleman with but one fault—a sharp wit combined with a certain insensitivity. Katharine then notes that Dumain is "a well-accomplished youth" of great virtue, but, because he is quite ignorant of evil, he is in some respects dangerous since he can accidentally employ his virtues in the wrong way. Lastly, Rosaline talks of Biron and says that he is the most merry and gracious man she has ever met, who indulges in the finest conversation.

COMMENT: This scene gives character sketches of the young men and also sets up the pairings which we will see later in the play. Note that some of the speech assignments in this scene appear confused.

Boyet returns to tell the Princess that the King intends to pitch a tent for the French ladies rather than break his oath and invite them into his court. On the arrival of the King of Navarre, the Princess draws attention to his lack of hospitality. In the background, Rosaline and Biron renew their old acquaintance in stychomythic wit-combat. The Princess and the King then proceed to the subject of the diplomatic mission. The King of France offers to pay half his debt to Navarre, 100,000 crowns, for which the French province of Aquitaine is to be collateral (security). Navarre, however, holds out for the full sum and says that Aquitaine is insufficient security for the loan. He would prefer to give up his rights in Aquitaine in exchange for the discharge of the debt.

> **COMMENT:**   There may be an historical basis for this incident, the negotiations between Charles VI and the King of Navarre in 1420 for the same amount of money, or those between Catherine de Médicis and Henry of Navarre in 1586 concerning Aquitaine. Perhaps, too, it may concern an embassy by Marguerite de Valois to her estranged husband in 1579 concerning her dowry. Evidence is scanty.

The Princess claims that the entire debt has been paid, but the King replies that he has not seen the money. In return, the Princess offers to produce papers proving payment signed by the King's father, but, since the papers have not yet arrived, the Princess and her retinue must remain overnight in the vicinity. However, the King will not break his vow and admit the ladies to his house. During this time, the wit-combat of Rosaline and Biron has continued, and Longaville and Dumain have surreptitiously inquired after the other two ladies in the company. The vow seems very close to dissolution, especially when Boyet notes that the King is completely smitten with the Princess herself.

COMMENT AND SUMMARY: This act furthers the plot by showing that the young men of the court are just as struck with the young ladies as the Frenchwomen are with the lords. The diplomatic proceedings are important mainly as a device to get everyone together. Obviously, the main interest in the play, and this act, is love. Note the continual playing with rhyme in the verbal fencing among members of the court. Rosaline and Biron are particularly adept at the game in this scene.

ACT III: SCENE 1

In another part of the park, Armado calls for his page to sing to him, a request that proves that the Don is in the throes of love-melancholy. Music is always considered highly suitable for Elizabethan lovers: it could both soothe and prolong the passion. Armado and Moth then engage in another wit-combat, this time concerning love and the probable status of the virtue of Jaquenetta. In his desperation, Armado tells Moth to release Costard so that the rustic may act as a messenger and carry a letter to Jaquenetta. When Costard arrives, we have another scene in which the clown mistakes the word in his literal, but obtuse, way.

After Armado and Moth depart, Biron enters and gives Costard another letter which is to be delivered to Rosaline. Like Armado, he gives the clown a shilling, a larger remuneration than that of the Spaniard, which causes wonder in Costard. Biron then speaks of his passion and he ruefully considers the depth of his fall. He, who had always been cynical about love and who had always made fun of the extravagances of lovers, is now, himself, in love. He tries to claim that he is a woman-hater, but he is then forced to admit the power of love by noticing that he loves the most ugly woman of all: a dark-haired lady with a pale skin and black eyes. Further, she is a lady who would gratify her physical passion without thinking twice.

> COMMENT: To the Elizabethans, a dark lady was not considered beautiful. They saw beauty as coming from light golden hair, gray or blue eyes, a fair, rosy complexion, white teeth, and a high noble forehead. Rosaline, like Cleopatra, does not qualify. The suggestion of passion in Rosaline may possibly be allied to the dark lady of Shakespeare's sonnets, but an accurate source is yet to be found.

Biron again attacks himself for loving such an unfit lady, but concludes with an act of resignation: he will undergo all the punishments of love-melancholy; he will write poems, pray, plead, and groan. Such is his fate —some men will love ladies, and some, the mere servant girl.

SUMMARY: This scene has several important functions in defining love and in advancing the plot.

1. By placing two aspects of love-melancholy next to each other, Shakespeare has managed to achieve a contrast between the false, physical passion of Armado and the sincere, honest passion of the reluctant Biron.

2. Shakespeare pokes fun at the tortures of lovers in general.

3. Costard now becomes essential for the advancement of the plot, because, obviously, the letters can be confused. Indeed, as we learn later in the play, this is precisely what happens.

ACT IV: SCENE 1

The Princess, her ladies, and Boyet now enter the scene, which is, as before, a portion of the park of the King of Navarre. This time the entire group is going shooting, and the Princess amuses herself by being witty at the expense of the Forester who has been assigned to lead them.

> COMMENT: Probably some kind of comparison is implied between the Princess of France and Diana, the chaste goddess of the hunt. Certainly, the Princess shows herself as a very independent lady for a lord to marry. The Princess's jokes at the expense of the Forester represent a normal contemporary relationship between various classes and should not be interpreted as cruel.

Costard then enters and delivers a letter from Monsieur Biron to the lady Rosaline which the Princess orders Boyet to open and read aloud to the company. As he takes it, Boyet notes that it is addressed to Jaquenetta, but, since the ladies wish to hear it, he reads it aloud. Of course, it is the carefully composed letter of Don Adriano de Armado and it is full of quaint words, classical references, rhetorical devices, puns, questions, even a snatch of Latin. The ladies are highly amused.

> **COMMENT:**   In the character of Don Armado, and, particularly, in this letter, Shakespeare seems to be parodying *the vices of Elizabethan writing*. The writers of the time, Shakespeare included, were highly conscious of the arts of rhetoric and of figurative writing. They were also passionately interested in the resources of the English language which they were constantly expanding and developing.

The rest of this scene is concerned with joking at the expense of Costard, Rosaline, and the absent Biron.

SUMMARY: This scene represents the beginning of the real love complications of the play. Note that they begin with a very simple dramatic device—the confusion of two letters. Again, the basis of the comedy here is literary and linguistic. The Princess exercises her wit; then, by contrast, Don Armado's letter shows the ponderous and pedantic nature of his mind.

ACT IV: SCENE 2

This scene, like the others, takes place in the park. Here we meet two new personages in Holofernes, the schoolteacher, and Sir Nathaniel, the curate. Dull accompanies them; his ignorance serves as a whetstone for their wit.

> **COMMENT:**   Since Holofernes and Sir Nathaniel have little to do with the plot itself, attempts have been made to see them as portraits of persons well known at the time. None of the suggestions is completely acceptable, although there are some specific comments later in the play which would seem to indicate that actual persons are portrayed. Holofernes' chief comic device is his continual mingling of Latin and English.

Holofernes proceeds to impress Sir Nathaniel by reciting a poem full of *alliteration* (words beginning with the same letter), puns, and carefully logical development of theme. Dull is confused by the words a few more times until Jaquenetta arrives accompanied by Costard. A rather strange exchange concerning "piercing a hogshead" takes place. This conversation may have something to do with the Nashe-Harvey controversy, but the parallel is by no means certain. Jaquenetta wants the Curate to read her letter to her because she cannot read (which makes Armado's passion for her the more amusing). After showing off his learning, Holofernes settles down to listen while Nathaniel reads the sonnet written by Biron which should, of course, have gone to Rosaline.

COMMENT: The sonnet (IV.ii.109-122) was printed in a collection of poems, *The Passionate Pilgrim* (1599), containing poems by writers other than Shakespeare. The collection includes two other sonnets which appear in this play.

After hearing the sonnet, Holofernes criticizes the way in which Sir Nathaniel read the poem, going on to say that he is not very impressed with the sonnet itself. He then questions Jaquenetta and sees that the letter is, in fact, addressed to the Lady Rosaline. He promptly sends Jaquenetta, with the letter, to the King.

SUMMARY: This scene serves both to introduce new characters and to advance the plot.

1. It introduces two more highly literary characters in Nathaniel and Holofernes, who are, possibly, portraits of real people.

2. It completes the confusion of the two letters, one from Biron to Rosaline and the other from Armado to Jaquenetta.

3. It reveals the love of Biron to the audience—knowledge which is important in comprehending the next scene because of Biron's previous remarks deriding love.

ACT IV: SCENE 3

Biron enters with a paper and bitterly laments his fate of falling in love with Rosaline. Obviously, he is the complete victim of love-melancholy; now he wishes that his three companions were also in love. As if in answer to his wish, the King appears with a paper. Biron conceals himself and listens as his lord reads a sixteen-line sonnet-like poem in which the language becomes very contrived. Suddenly, the King sees Longaville approaching with a paper, and he, too, hides. Longaville begins by expressing his love for Maria; then he commences to read a sonnet. In the background, Biron continues to make sharp comments about love and Longaville's expression of the passion. He criticizes Longaville's poetic talent until Dumain appears, also with a paper. By this time, the three young gentlemen are busy making fun of Dumain who reads a twenty-line poem in rhyming couplets telling of the manner in which love struck him.

COMMENT: The sonnet of Longaville (IV.iii.60-74) and the poem of Dumain (IV.iii.101-120) both appear in *The Passionate Pilgrim.*

Longaville then reveals himself and announces that he has heard Dumain break his vow. Then the King, himself, steps forward and chides both Longaville and Dumain, making fun of their respective poems. At this moment, Biron, secures in his ignorance of the whereabouts of his own sonnet, comes out of hiding to reprove the three of them as oath-breakers. He holds himself up as the only person among them who has had the courage to hold to a vow once taken, and declares that he is impervious to the passion of love. But his bubble of pride is soon pricked with the arrival of Jaquenetta and Costard carrying his poem to Rosaline. Biron recognizes it when it is given to him to read and he promptly tears it up. But his companions discover the identity of the writer and Biron, too, must admit his passion.

> **COMMENT:** This part of the scene is very well composed with its contrasting comments from each lover. It also builds to a good climax with the discovery of Biron's passion.

The King, Longaville, and Dumain then ridicule Biron, who defends the beauty of his lady, in particular, her dark hair and eyes. But black, according to the King, "is the badge of hell, the hue of dungeons and the suit of night."

> **COMMENT:** The quarto and folio texts read "school of night," and some critics hold that it may refer to a group of young men of the time who are thought to have been engaged in scientific, literary, and poetic work which was suspected of being atheistic. The group may also have included Christopher Marlowe and Sir Walter Raleigh. Again, evidence is scanty.

Then, at the request of the King, Biron attempts with adroit, at times, fallacious, reasoning to prove that the three young men have not broken their oath. He claims that in swearing to study, they have forsworn the only real books there are: the eyes of ladies. After this argument is enthusiastically received, the four young men joyously resolve to woo the French ladies with "revels, dances, masks, and merry hours."

COMMENT AND SUMMARY: This admirably constructed scene unmasks all the young men as lovers, and shows the impossibility of their vows in their fantastic behavior. Human nature cannot be denied, and men and women will always fall in love, despite all the prohibitions of society or voluntary vows. The play has now disposed of the vow to study, and the last act will be concerned with the wooing of the ladies.

ACT V: SCENE 1

This scene in the park opens with the meeting of Holofernes, Sir Nathaniel, and Dull, who are discussing Don Adriano de Armado. Holofernes pedantically complains about the way the Don "draweth out the thread of his verbosity finer than the staple of his argument," and then goes on to reprove him further for the way in which he leaves some letters silent, for example, "debt" and "calf." Here again Shakespeare is making fun of pedants in general and a new movement in English pronunciation in particular. At this point, the Spaniard himself appears, accompanied by Moth and Costard. He talks with Holofernes, while Moth and Costard make fun of their pedantry until finally Costard produces the longest word ever: *honorificabilitudinitatibus*.

> **COMMENT:** Shakespeare here seems to be using Costard as a

mouthpiece instead of a consistent character. It is indeed odd that a rustic clown who habitually mistakes the use of the word should be capable of pronouncing this monster.

Armado and Holofernes continue talking and in their personal remarks they become so specific that one suspects Shakespeare of making topical references. Armado then suggests, in his characteristically involved language, that they present an entertainment to the French ladies. Holofernes agrees, suggesting the Pageant of the Nine Worthies.

COMMENT: The Nine Worthies were traditionally three pagan, three Jewish, and three Christian heroes: Hector of Troy, Alexander the Great, and Julius Caesar; Joshua, (the conqueror of Jericho), David, and Judas Maccabaeus; Arthur, Charlemagne, and Godfrey of Bouillon (the leader of the First Crusade).

The parts are assigned casually and the scene concludes.

COMMENT AND SUMMARY: This scene acts as a bridge between two different aspects of the play. The description of the pageant is essential because the nobles make such fun of it later on. The scene also manages to derive further amusement from the pedantic vices of some Elizabethan writers.

ACT V: SCENE 2

Elsewhere in the park, the Princess and her ladies are discussing the gifts they have received. But there is some sorrow, too, because Katharine, one of the ladies, recalls the way her sister died of love-melancholy. The Princess has received a brooch with the design of a lady surrounded by diamonds and a poem from the King. Rosaline has received a poem and an unidentified gift from Biron. Dumain has sent Katharine a pair of gloves and a poem, and Longaville has given Maria a chain of pearls plus a poem. Boyet then arrives to tell the ladies that the gentlemen are on their way to visit them—but for some reason they have come disguised in Russian dress.

COMMENT: Perhaps this Russian disguise had some contemporary significance. Russians had come to the court of Henry VIII many years earlier. Also, in 1594-95, the characters of Russians and Negroes had appeared in a dramatic performance. But, possibly, these disguises merely reflected general Elizabethan interest in these groups and countries.

The ladies decide to make the young men work hard to gain their affection. They mask themselves and exchange articles of clothing so that the young men woo the wrong girls. The King woos Rosaline, while Biron makes love to the Princess. Similarly, Dumain woos Maria, and Longaville, Katharine. The ladies make merciless fun of the lovesick young men who finally withdraw. The ladies make merry over their joke, and are soon given another chance because the gentlemen reappear in their usual dress.

At first the ladies make fun of the wooing of the 'Muscovites," but, gradually, they let the young men in on the joke. The most notable reaction comes from Biron who swears that he will stop trying to woo in high-flown and complicated language and will be more blunt and direct in "russet yeas and honest kersey noes." This technique may be more effective.

> **COMMENT:** This statement seems to indicate Shakespeare's poor opinion of the high-flown language and poetic passion of all the young men. At the same time, he may be commenting on the pedantic pageant which is about to take place.

Costard then arrives with the Pageant of the Nine Worthies. The courtiers of France and Navarre are highly amused by the entertainment; they make fun of almost every word. Boyet and Biron are so witty that the pageant barely gets started. Humor based on language abounds here.

> **COMMENT:** This idea of a pageant presented by persons of a lower class to courtiers was quite common in Elizabethan times. The jokes at the expense of the unlearned are not meant to be cruel.

The merriment reaches its height with the accusation that Don Armado has got Jaquenetta with child. Suddenly, the laughter is interrupted by the arrival of Mercade, a French courtier, with the sad news that the French King is dead. Biron dismisses the pageant; all the players leave. The Princess announces her intention to leave immediately for France.

> **COMMENT:** This sudden intrusion of sorrow is unusual at the end of a Shakespearean comedy. It probably is meant to represent the reality of life in which gladness cannot exist forever, but is always clouded by sorrow.

The unhappy news forces everyone into action and the King asks the Princess and her ladies to grant the suit of the gentlemen of Navarre. Biron, in plain speech, admits that they have all broken their vows, but, since the motivation for this was love, the ladies must share the guilt. In answer, the Princess declares that there is and has been too little time to make a final decision. She reproves the King for making and breaking his oath so quickly and tells him to go into a hermitage and lead a retired and solitary life for a year in order to test his love. He must also do penance for having denied, even temporarily, the society of ladies. If, at the end of that time, he is still of the same mind, then she will be his. Both Katharine and Maria tell Dumain and Longaville that they, too, must wait a year before the ladies give their consent. Rosaline, however, imposes a more difficult penance on Biron. He must spend a year in a hospital where he must endeavor to jest and amuse the sick because, not only has his tongue been very sharp, but he has been the most outspoken foe of love.

> **COMMENT:** Note that the sense of lines V.ii.827-832 is repeated

in an expanded version in V.ii.851-881. This oversight possibly indicates revision of the text.

So the young gentlemen do not acquire their ladies at the end of the play, something that makes *Love's Labour's Lost* an unusual comedy. Armado returns to say that he, too, has sworn to perform a test: he will become a farmer for three years in order to win Jaquenetta. He then asks if the company would like to hear a song about the owl and cuckoo which Holofernes and Sir Nathaniel have composed. The King approves, and the two pedants, accompanied by Costard and the others, arrive. Then they sing one of Shakespeare's most pleasant songs, which is also one of his most realistic ones. The seasons of Spring and Winter tell of their comforts and discomforts, but each stanza (unit of verse) ends with a refrain suggesting the infidelity of wives: "Cuckoo, cuckoo; O word of fear,/ Unpleasing to a married ear."

> **COMMENT:** The spirit of this song sums up the bittersweet tone of the play; yet it seems an afterthought. It is not the kind of song one would have expected the pedants to compose. The "cuckoo" refrain is, of course, a skeptical pun on the word "cuckold," (a husband whose wife is unfaithful to him who is customarily pictured as having horns. The cuckold was *a figure of fun* in the Elizabethan theatre.

SUMMARY: This scene is notable for the way in which it adds to the complications and completely changes the tone of the play.

1. It combines three different threads of action: the love affairs of the courtly folk, the pedantic comedy, and the sadness of death which intrudes into the world of merriment, love, and escape.

2. The tricks played on the lovers foreshadow the final test they are all asked to submit to.

3. The young men realize that true love cannot be denied, and that it is impossible to avoid women, even by making a vow. All learning and all actions are, in effect, given meaning and purpose through love.

4. The subplot of the peasants and Jaquenetta contrasts the physical passion of love with the spiritual and intellectual passion of the courtly folk.

5. The final test of the courtly lovers is designed to remove the purely physical attraction from the love-relationship and thereby to purify their passion.

6. The concluding poem returns to the motif of sensual love and shows that it can be accompanied by infidelity. At the same time, the poem portrays realistically the details of the seasons in the English countryside.

CHARACTER ANALYSES:
"LOVE'S LABOUR'S LOST"

On the whole, the characters of this play are not fully drawn. They engage our intellect rather than our sympathy, and, in this regard, should be considered pure comic characters.

THE KING: Ferdinand, King of Navarre, at first believes very firmly in the superiority of the mind over the passions. In his idealism, he proposes the vow that the young men retire from the society of women in order to study and develop their minds. At first, he also is a shrewd bargainer with the Princess, but he soon falls in love and eventually writes poetry to her. He is finally forced to admit that he is wrong and must do penance for having denied the worth of love.

BIRON: He is the most interesting young man at the court of Navarre, and is important because he is the first of Shakespeare's scoffers at love who all, of course, later fall deeply in love. In some ways, he is the wisest of the gentlemen because he sees the problems involved in keeping the vow, but he has great pride in his own ability to keep it. He is cynical and realistic in most of his attitudes, but there is a bitter streak in his wit that Rosaline later punishes him for. When he falls in love, he ironically picks the lady Rosaline, whose wit is nearly equal to his own, and whose beauty is not the kind generally idealized by the Elizabethans. He is also clever in his use of words and makes many witty remarks that are based on a knowledge of the resources of language. He is a capable thinker, and, in a brilliant manner, he manages to prove that learning without the love of women is nothing at all because the truest learning begins in the study of a lady's eyes.

DON ADRIANO DE ARMADO: This pedantic Spaniard has fantastic pretensions to learning and to rhetorical brilliance. "He draweth out the thread of his verbosity finer than the staple of his argument." At the same time, Shakespeare reveals his pretense for what it is by having him fall in love with the illiterate country dairymaid, Jaquenetta. The resolution of this subplot shows that physical passion in this play is meant to be reproved. Armado is also a parody of some of the vices of language common in Elizabethan England, and some critics have thought him a comic portrait of Gabriel Harvey, the Cambridge scholar.

HOLOFERNES: He is excellently drawn as the pedantic schoolmaster, and, since we are told that he taught in a schoolhouse on the top of a particular hill, Shakespeare may have been giving us hints of Holofernes' identity. Unfortunately, they are meaningless today. His importance lies in the way in which he uses words and continually tries to impress the Curate with his learning. He has very little, indeed, to do with the main plot of the play, except to read Jaquenetta's letter. The Pageant of the Nine Worthies is supposed to be his composition, as is the last song which is certainly not composed in his usual style.

SIR NATHANIEL: The Curate is extremely impressed with Holofernes' learning. He is a kind of echo-figure, and is a fine example of a hero-worshipper. He is supposed to have helped compose the final song.

MOTH: He is the witty young page to Don Armado who engages in verbal fencing with his master. Sometimes, he outdoes Armado in his witticisms. Some critics see him as a portrait of Thomas Nashe, the Cambridge man and writer.

COSTARD: He is the rustic clown, as opposed to the witty page. It is he who is originally caught with Jaquenetta. His chief comic device is the misuse of words and the mistaking of their meaning. The nobles make great sport of him, beginning with his name which means a kind of apple and is also a slang term for the head.

ANTHONY DULL: He is the first of Shakespeare's wildly inefficient constables who think they are learned, but who have great difficulty in their use, or rather misuse, of language.

LONGAVILLE: He is a gentleman of Navarre who woos Maria. He is a fine gentleman, well learned in the arts and valiant in arms. Unfortunately, he is rather insensitive to the feelings of others.

DUMAIN: He is another gentleman of Navarre. He, too, is "well-accomplished" and overly virtuous. But, because he is so virtuous, he sometimes fails to recognize evil in trying to put the best face on the actions of others. He woos Katharine.

THE PRINCESS OF FRANCE: Both beautiful and witty, she is a shrewd bargainer in matters of both property and love as the King of Navarre finds out to his cost. She is clever enough to recognize the symptoms of love in her ladies, and realistic enough to see that young men who change their minds so rapidly ought not to be trusted immediately. She, therefore, tests them in the scene of disguised wooing. Later she sends her own lover, the King, to a hermitage for a year to prove his constancy.

ROSALINE: She is the wittiest of the three ladies of the French court. She is not considered beautiful in the conventional Elizabethan manner because of her black hair, black eyes, and pale complexion. In some ways, she possesses some of the traits of the "dark lady" of Shakespeare's sonnet cycle. She is wooed by Biron, but she seems the most hardhearted of the ladies because she sends her lover to jest in a hospital for a year. This action is, nevertheless, sensible. Biron, as the chief scoffer at love, has committed more errors to do penance for, and he also needs to develop his generosity and to cultivate a sympathetic heart.

KATHARINE AND MARIA: These are the two other ladies of the French court. Katharine is the red-gold beauty who is the gentlest of them all, possibly because she saw her sister die of love-melancholy. She is wooed by Dumain. Maria, in contrast to Katharine, is more blunt towards her wooer, Longaville.

BOYET AND MERCADE: Boyet is the chaperon of the French ladies and the Princess's diplomatic adviser. He is witty and enjoys the discomfiture of the lovers. Together with Biron, he makes merry remarks at the expense of the Pageant of the Nine Worthies.

Mercade is not characterized. He merely brings bad news; as the messenger, he represents the intrusion of the real world with its trials and grief into the world of the witty lovers.

ESSAY QUESTIONS FOR REVIEW: "LOVE'S LABOUR'S LOST"

1. What are the major attitudes towards love in this play?

Basically, there are three entirely separate attitudes. The first is that of the young men of Navarre, they believe that love can be denied. They decide to spend three years away from the society of ladies, but, the moment that the ladies of France appear, the gentlemen of Navarre fall in love with them. However, within the court, there are subdivisions of love. The King of Navarre, Dumain, and Longaville admit their love more readily, but they also take the oath to abjure ladies more willingly than does Biron. He is a man who seems to possess common sense, but he is a more cynical scoffer at love than his companions. He falls further than any of the others, because he chooses a lady who does not have any of the accepted signs of outward beauty.

The ladies of France have a slightly different view. Judging by what they say when they originally discuss the gentlemen of Navarre, the Princess sees readily that they are all in love with the men they describe. They admit their love less hesitatingly than do the young men; at the same time, they are not so hasty as the courtiers of Navarre. When the ladies see that the men speedily switch their allegiance from study to love they are rightly suspicious. The Princess, who can use her mourning as a good excuse, tells the King that he must do penance for a year in a hermitage for having attempted to renounce love. The other ladies impose similar penances on their lovers, with the exception of Rosaline who gives Biron, her gentleman, a much stiffer punishment. As he has been the greatest scoffer at love, so his privations must be greater. She sends him to jest all year in a hospital where he will learn sympathy and understanding so that he will be a better husband for her. The ladies, indeed, have reason to test the constancy of such wavering persons.

The third attitude towards love is that of Don Adriano de Armado, Costard, and Jaquenetta. Their view of love is entirely physical, and when the Don falls for the illiterate dairymaid, this attitude becomes obvious. By the end of the play, he, too, is doing penance; however, it is not a spiritual or intellectual penance, but a physical one. He has promised to follow the plough for three years to win Jaquenetta. In this way, he also will pay for his intellectual pretensions.

Since none of the gentlemen actually attain their ladies at the end of the play it is aptly named *Love's Labour's Lost*. They all have to work to prove themselves worthy of their ladies and to purge themselves of their past faults. Therefore, the final view of love in the play is an exalted one, and the limited physical passion of Don Armado is considered blameworthy.

2. What attitudes towards study are there in this play?

There are two main attitudes towards study in this play, and, by the end of the play, they are reconciled. The first is that study is meant to be a discipline which is removed from the affairs of the everyday world. It is difficult and it aims at spiritual and abstract knowledge, such as philosophy. It requires an almost cloistered existence, and ladies are rigidly excluded from such a little academe which is not concerned with mundane affairs.

Such is the view of the King and all of his court, except Biron, who questions this concept of study and complains about the strictness of the rules. Then, when all the young men discover that they are in love, Biron shows at great length, with ingenious reasoning, that the truest study lies in women's eyes. Therefore, one cannot give up life entirely for the purpose of study, because mental discipline must be tempered with virtuous and ideal love. True education needs true love on the part of both men and women.

3. How is this play constructed, and what are its most frequently employed comic devices?

The play is divided into two sections: the main plot, dealing with the difficulties of the courtly characters; and the subplot, dealing with the affair of Don Armado and Jaquenetta. The comic devices in the main plot are largely concerned with literary material, such as the writing of sonnets, and they are highly intellectual, particularly in Biron's reasoning on study and love. Similarly, the ladies of France pun and play upon words. The subplot is concerned with two kinds of humor which are also based on verbal wit. We have the pseudobrilliant rhetorical style of Armado, Sir Nathaniel, and Holofernes, together with the rustic and semiliterate humor of Costard. The play is unusual in that it *ends in sorrow* although it is a comedy. But the conclusion parallels the beginning: the world of sorrow and pain must intrude into the world of love, just as love intruded into the world of study.

"THE MERRY WIVES OF WINDSOR"

THE PLAY: *The Merry Wives of Windsor,* an offshoot from the historical play, *Henry IV,* has an interesting legend. In the eighteenth century, it was said that the play had been written hurriedly in fourteen days because Queen Elizabeth had expressed a desire to see Falstaff in love. Today, we are inclined to doubt the truth of this statement, but we do accept the suggestion that the play was written swiftly. For instance, there are odd sections of the subplots which are never developed—the business of the horse-stealers in Act IV, and the revenge of Sir Hugh and Doctor Caius on the Host in Act III are examples. There are also strange, imprecise connections with the Order of the Garter which have recently been discussed and which may help establish the date of the play as having been first performed in April 1597. Apparently, too, there are topical references to people known to the courtly audience which first saw the play whom we cannot now identify with certainty. The persons of the play are middle-class, and the setting is England in Shakespeare's day. The play itself depends largely upon comic situation and on the characters turning the tables on each other. There is little philosophical and intellectual content; the central theme of the play is love—the punishment of a dishonest passion and the triumph of sincere, true love over all obstacles. And, for the occasion, delicate compliments are paid both to the Queen and to the courtiers having the Order of the Garter who were probably in the first audience to see the play.

SOURCE AND TEXT: The play is an Italianate comedy in structure and situations, but no specific source has been established for the entire action. Several parallel situations have been found, but nothing definitive. Most scholars think that, if there was a single source, it was an earlier dramatic work, now lost.

The text, however, is the greatest puzzle of all. The play was first printed in 1602 in a text that seems highly confused and corrupt, but was not reprinted until the First Folio of 1623. The second text has certainly undergone revision, it is about 1,000 lines longer than the quarto text of 1602. Possibly, the quarto was a reconstruction from memory by someone who had some acquaintance with the original text because the cutting of so many lines would seem to be too drastic for an abridgement.

THE PLOT: Sir John Falstaff and his companions, Bardolph, Nym, and Pistol, have been disturbing the property of Shallow, a Justice of the Peace in Gloucestershire. The Justice threatens to bring a suit against Falstaff, but Master Page talks the men out of it by inviting them to dinner.

Page has a daughter named Anne whom the Justice, with the help of Sir Hugh Evans, the Welsh parson, wants to marry to his cousin, Abraham Slender. But there are other candidates for Anne's hand: Doctor Caius, the French doctor, and Master Fenton, a penniless gentleman who was formerly the companion of Prince Hal. Although Slender is Master Page's choice, Doctor Caius is the choice of Mistress Page. Anne, however, loves Fenton. All three wooers ask Mistress Quickly for help and she accepts money from all of them for her services. But when Doctor Caius finds out that he has a rival in Slender, who is supported by Sir Hugh Evans, he challenges the parson to a duel. The Host of the Garter Inn, however, sends them both to opposite ends of the town; finally, the duel is called off without much persuasion being necessary.

While at Page's house, Sir John Falstaff has become attracted to Mistress Ford and also to Mistress Page. Consequently, he writes identical love letters to both of them. He tells Pistol and Nym to deliver the letters to the ladies, but, for some reason, they develop scruples and refuse. Falstaff then sends them away. He has already sent Bardolph away because he was unable to pay him. The messages are taken by Falstaff's page while Pistol and Nym decide to get revenge on Falstaff by telling Masters Ford and Page of the knight's designs on their wives.

When Mistress Ford and Mistress Page receive their identical love letters they decide to teach Falstaff a lesson, so Mistress Ford invites him to visit the next day. In the meantime, Ford has begun to fear that his wife may yield to Falstaff's persuasion, but Page, in contrast, thinks the whole thing is very funny and trusts his wife entirely. Ford, however, disguises himself, using the name Brook, visits Falstaff, and gives him money to see if the knight can manage to make Mistress Ford available for him. This is his way of testing the virtue of his wife. He then enlists the help of his friends to catch his wife with Falstaff, since the fat man has told him of his own proposed meeting with Mistress Ford the next day.

Just as Falstaff starts to woo Mistress Ford, her friend, Mistress Page, brings news that Ford is about to enter the house. Falstaff jumps into a convenient laundry basket full of dirty clothes and is carried out of the house, past the suspicious Ford and—dumped into a muddy stream at Datchet-mead, as the merry wives had planned. Elated at the success of their trick, the ladies decide to try another, so they send a message to Falstaff suggesting another meeting with Mistress Ford early the next morning. Again, Ford in disguise visits Falstaff who tells him of the proposed meeting, and, once again, Ford gets ready to catch his wife with the knight. The next morning Falstaff and Mistress Ford are again together when Mistress Page rushes in to announce the forthcoming arrival of Ford. This time the ladies hustle Falstaff upstairs and dress him in a gown belonging to the Witch of Brentford, the aunt of Mistress Ford's maid. When Ford sees the disguised Falstaff, he thinks that he is the one woman he hates with desperation so he beats the fat man out of the house, as he had threatened the old woman he would do to her. The ladies then tell their husbands of their jokes at Falstaff's expense and suggest that a last attempt be made to teach the fat knight a lesson.

The wives invite him to come disguised with horns as the ghost of Herne the Hunter and meet them at Herne's Oak in Windsor Forest. Mistress Anne Page will be disguised as a fairy and children will be brought in to play the parts of her subjects. Once Falstaff appears, this company will call upon him to explain why he, a sinful man, is present in their haunts, and they will then pinch and burn him until he screams for mercy. Master Page sees this business of disguise at midnight on a dark night as a good opportunity to send Anne, dressed in white, with Slender to be secretly married. Mistress Page has the same idea. She tells her candidate, Doctor Caius, that Anne will be dressed in green, and she suggests that he steal her away and marry her in secret. But Fenton has enlisted the help of the Host to arrange for a vicar to marry Anne and himself secretly. And so it all works out. Slender and Caius both steal away with disguised boys, Falstaff is pinched black and blue, Mistress Anne marries the man she loves, the honor of the merry wives is preserved, and Ford learns not to suspect his wife.

DETAILED SUMMARY OF "THE MERRY WIVES OF WINDSOR"

ACT I: SCENES 1-2

The first scene opens in front of George Page's house in Windsor. The time is contemporary. Justice Robert Shallow, Abraham Slender, his cousin, and Sir Hugh Evans, a Welsh parson, enter. Shallow, Justice of the Peace in the county of Gloucester, is angry with Sir John Falstaff and his cronies who have been ruining his property. Shallow's opinions are seconded by his cousin Slender, who notes the lineage of the Justice, referring carefully to his coat of arms with its three luces, or freshwater fish.

> COMMENT: One critic (J. Leslie Hotson) identifies Shallow as a portrait of William Gardiner, a justice in Surrey, and his stepson William Wayte, with whom Shakespeare was bound over to keep the peace. Gardiner's coat of arms seems to be the one here described. The passage has also been thought to give rise to the legend of Shakespeare's having stolen deer from the park of Sir Thomas Lucy, and, as a result, having to leave Stratford in a hurry.

Sir Hugh Evans tries very hard to calm Shallow; his comments are delivered with a marked Welsh accent.

> COMMENT: This play is notable for the humorous use of dialect and the "hacked" English of both Evans and Caius, the Frenchman.

Evans manages to talk Shallow out of starting a lawsuit because of Falstaff's actions. Then he discusses the possibility of a marriage between Master Abraham Slender and Mistress Anne Page. Slender immediately remembers the financial position of the girl: she has been left seven hundred pounds by her grandmother, and her father will also leave her money. Indeed, the girl is a good match, as Evans points out. Master Page, Anne's father, then arrives and says that he would like to reconcile the strife between Falstaff and Shallow.

The Justice insists that he has been wronged, but Page claims that Falstaff admits that fact. Nevertheless, Shallow remains angry when Falstaff, accompanied by Bardolph, Nym, and Pistol, appears. Shallow states his grievances, that Falstaff has beaten his men, killed his deer, and broken into his lodge. Falstaff admits the charges are true, but advises against Shallow's making a court case out of them. Pistol then denies the charge of having picked Slender's pocket, and Falstaff supports his companion.

At this point, Anne Page enters with wine, and is followed by Mistress Page and Mistress Ford. Master Page then invites everyone to dinner, asking them to drink together and to be reconciled. Slender, in the meantime, tries desperately to be left alone with Anne so that he may woo her. But in his earlier discussion with Shallow and Evans we have discovered that he is not really in love with Anne. He accidentally speaks of the "decrease" of love after marriage, and, in general, gives the impression that it will be a marriage of convenience.

> COMMENT: This play is full of occasions in which characters misuse words, picking ones which sound similar, but which may sometimes have opposite meanings. At the same time, Slender's speech expresses almost exactly the situation which often occurred when a loveless marriage for money was contracted.

Left alone with Anne, Slender refuses food, presumably because he thinks this is the required behavior of a lover, but all he can talk to the girl about is bear baiting, a subject not considered particularly suitable for ladies. Finally, he is forced by Page to come to dinner.

The next extremely brief scene follows immediately in the same place. Sir Hugh Evans sends Simple, Slender's page to Mistress Quickly, the servant to Doctor Caius, with a letter. The aim of the communication is to ask Mistress Quickly to speak to Mistress Anne on Slender's behalf.

SUMMARY: These opening scenes are, essentially, expository, and they also get the plot under way.

1. We meet Justice Shallow and learn of his grievance against Falstaff, which is soon satisfied.

2. We are introduced to Shallow's cousin, Slender, one of the wooers of Mistress Anne Page.

3. We meet Mistress Anne and find that she is a very wealthy match for a hopeful young man.

4. Sir Hugh Evans is set up as a prime mover in the plot to have Slender marry Anne Page. His heavy Welsh accent is established and we can expect further fun to be made of it, of Welshmen in general, and, in particular, of their reputed liking for cheese.

5. We meet George Page, a bluff, hearty, and peaceable man who is apparently well off financially.

6. We see Mistress Ford and Mistress Page, who we will later discover to be the merry wives of the title. They appear only briefly.

7. Falstaff, as rotund as ever, and his friends are introduced. They seem to be just as incorrigible as they were in the earlier history plays, and they are engaged in some rather rough illegal activities.

ACT I: SCENE 3

This scene takes place in a room at the Garter Inn at Windsor a short time later. Falstaff announces that he is running short of funds, therefore, he must send away some of his company. The Host immediately offers to employ Bardolph as a tapster (barman) to which Bardolph and Falstaff agree. After Bardolph departs, Falstaff says that he is not sorry to see him go, since his thefts had been rather too open of late.

Falstaff changes the subject abruptly by expressing his intention of making love to Mistress Ford. He shows one letter that he has written to the lady, and another to Mistress Page, who, according to Falstaff had encouraged him in the same way as Mistress Ford. Perhaps there is a hint of Falstaff's real intent when he notes that Mistress Page "bears the purse too; she is a region in Guiana, all gold and bounty." Possibly, he wishes to recoup his finances. To Falstaff's surprise, however, Pistol and Nym both refuse to take the letters; for some reason, they have become self-righteous. In a fit of annoyance, Falstaff tells his page, Robin, to do the errand and he sends his former friends away. After Falstaff and his page leave, Nym and Pistol decide to get revenge on their old master by telling Masters Page and Ford of his plans against their wives' virtue.

SUMMARY: This scene is used primarily for the advancement of the plot.

1. It establishes the situation by informing us about the letters with which Falstaff woos Mistress Ford and Mistress Page.

2. It shows Falstaff as short of money; therefore, it gives him some motivation for the trick he is about to play.

3. By having Pistol and Nym refuse to take the letters, Falstaff is given an excuse for turning them away.

4. Since they have been dismissed, Nym and Pistol are given a motive for revenge which they effect by telling the husbands of the ladies that Falstaff intends to solicit of his plan. In this manner, the complication of the plot is begun.

ACT I: SCENE 4

This scene takes place in a room at Doctor Caius's house. Mistress Quickly enters with Simple and John Rugby, Caius's manservant. Simple has delivered his message and Mistress Quickly promises to help Slender's suit of Mistress Anne. The moment Caius is heard, Mistress Quickly hides Simple in a cupboard, and then the Doctor himself, using a heavy French accent, arrives. He is in a great hurry because he must get to court on a "grande affaire."

> **COMMENT:** Caius is, perhaps, referring to the feast of the Order of the Garter for which this play was probably written. The Garter is the highest order of knighthood in England; its motto is *Honi soit qui mal y pense* (Shamed be he who thinks evil of it). The Chapel of the Order is at Windsor Castle. [*See*: William Green, bibliography.]

Simple is, however, discovered, and he tells Caius that Hugh Evans has sent him on Slender's behalf. In anger, Caius challenges Evans to a duel because the learned doctor himself wishes to wed Anne Page. Quickly tells Simple that Anne does not love the Frenchman.

No sooner have all the men departed than Master Fenton, a gentleman, enters and speaks with Mistress Quickly about *his* suit of Anne Page. Quickly claims that it is going well, and that Anne loves him; but, after Fenton has left his money with Quickly and gone away, we discover that she believes just the opposite.

COMMENT AND SUMMARY: By the end of this scene, most of the principal complications concerning Anne Page are set up.

1. Slender wishes to marry her for her money. He is assisted by Sir Hugh Evans, the Welsh parson.

2. Caius, the French doctor, also wishes to marry Anne, but Quickly says Anne does not care for him. Caius challenges Evans to a duel over the girl.

3. Fenton, a gentleman, also wishes to marry Anne. Quickly first tells him that Anne loves him, but denies the fact when she is alone.

4. Mistress Quickly is acting as go-between for all three suitors and, apparently, is being paid by all of them.

ACT II: SCENE 1

This scene takes place before the house of Master Page. Mistress Page enters carrying a letter. She is quite indignant that Sir John Falstaff has had the boldness to write her the love letter which she reads aloud. Then she insults Sir John, concluding with a wish to be avenged. No sooner has she finished than Mistress Ford enters and asks for advice. She begins by saying that, if she were prepared to go to hell for eternity, then she might be knighted. She then draws out Falstaff's letter and hands it to Mistress Page. To their joint amazement and chagrin, the two letters are identical. The merry wives are really incensed then, and they plot a joint revenge. Mistress Page seems to be the stronger personality in this scene, for Mistress Ford is concerned about the possible jealousy of her husband, while her companion says that her husband is so good that he is never jealous; furthermore, she would never give him cause to be.

No sooner have they left than Ford comes in with Pistol, and Page with Nym, and the two rogues reveal Falstaff's plans against their wives. Page, as his wife had expected, treats the whole thing as a joke, but Ford is less certain.

The two wives return, and when they encounter Mistress Quickly, they decide to use her as their messenger to Falstaff.

Left alone, Page and Ford discuss what they have heard, and, as Mistress Ford had predicted, her husband is quite disturbed by the situation, but Page trusts his wife completely.

> **COMMENT:** The unreasonably jealous husband was a conventional *figure of fun,* and his penalty usually was that his wife was unfaithful to him. At the same time, many Elizabethans believed in the natural moral weakness of women, using Eve as an example.

The Host, followed by Shallow, arrives, and the Justice announces that there is to be a duel between Sir Hugh and Doctor Caius. But he proceeds to tell the audience that the Host has sent the antagonists to opposite ends of the town to be sure that they will not meet.

Ford, who has been brooding for some time, asks the Host if he will introduce him to Falstaff under the name of Brook. The Host, who sees it as a merry joke, agrees. After the others leave, we discover that Ford has a different plan: he will test the honesty of his wife.

SUMMARY: This scene contains the following plot developments:

1. The two merry wives discover Falstaff's double dealing and plot revenge.

2. Pistol and Nym go ahead with their plan to warn Page and Ford.

3. The husbands behave as their wives predict: Page treats the news as a joke, but Ford is so distrustful of his wife's virtue that he decides to disguise himself as Brook and meet with Falstaff in order to discover what is going on between the knight and his wife.

4. The Host arranges to send Doctor Caius and Sir Hugh Evans to opposite ends of the town so that they will not be able to fight their duel.

ACT II: SCENE 2

This scene takes place in the Garter Inn and opens with Falstaff refusing to give Pistol a loan. Mistress Quickly then enters bringing a message from Mistress Ford which states that her husband will be absent from home between ten and eleven the next day. After a few comments on the jealousy of Ford, Mistress Quickly also delivers a message from Mistress Page in which that lady regrets that her husband is almost always home, but she says that she would like Falstaff to send his page, Robin, as a messenger since her husband has taken a fancy to the boy. Falstaff gives money to Quickly, who is obviously making a great profit out of the various operations she is running, and sends Robin to Mistress Page.

Ford is then announced, as Brook, and he tells Falstaff that he would dearly love to go to bed with Mistress Ford, but that the lady refuses him. Perhaps, he suggests, the knight might be more fortunate and more successful. Ford even gives Falstaff money to help him seduce her. The fat man, always willing to boast of his extraordinary prowess, promptly reveals the appointment Mistress Ford has made with him. Ford then asks whether Falstaff knows anything about the lady's husband, and he is justly rewarded for his suspicion and curiosity by hearing a very unflattering description of his own jealousy and his wife's virtue. The scene concludes with Ford's enraged soliloquy on the prospective infidelity of his wife in which he does not doubt she will indulge.

> **COMMENT:** Shakespeare here makes use of the comic possibilities of a husband who pays for his own cuckolding, and he also amuses the audience at the expense of the jealous husband who hears someone else's unflattering opinion of himself.

SUMMARY: This scene continues the plot of the merry wives against Falstaff, and that of Ford against his own wife.

1. Quickly brings messages to Falstaff from the ladies, and an appointment is arranged for the next day.

2. Ford, disguised as Brook, asks Falstaff for help in his own fictitious attempt to gain Mistress Ford for himself. He gives Falstaff money to test her virtue, and is, in effect, paying someone to make his own wife unfaithful to him.

ACT II: SCENE 3

This scene takes place in a field near Windsor where Doctor Caius and Jack Rugby, his servant, have been waiting "six or seven, two, tree hours" for the arrival of Sir Hugh Evans. Despite his bold talk, we can easily see that the Doctor is not very keen to fight anyone. His overestimate of the time he has been waiting indicates interesting possibilities either of his own late arrival, or of fear which makes the time seem longer. The Host, Shallow, Slender, and Page then tell Doctor Caius that Sir Hugh will certainly make him amends, and the Host promises to take Doctor Caius to a nearby farmhouse where Anne is said to be visiting.

COMMENT AND SUMMARY: This scene merely dramatizes the situation we have been told about in the preceding scene. It is meant to reveal Doctor Caius as a coward, and a bit of a braggart.

ACT III: SCENE 1

This scene is the counterpart of the previous one. It takes place in a field near Frogmore where Sir Hugh Evans and Simple are awaiting the arrival of Doctor Caius. Sir Hugh has sent Simple to many places to look for Caius, except to the right one, the town. He is speaking as boldly as Caius about what he will do, when Master Page, accompanied by Shallow and Slender, appears. They pretend not to know what is up, so Evans tells them. The Host, Caius, and Rugby then appear, and the two would-be duelists insult each other, each accusing the other of avoiding the appointment. Finally, the Host confesses his trick and invites everyone back to the Garter Inn for a drink, suggesting that the quarrel be made up. Caius and Sir Hugh agree, but, as they leave, the parson suggests the possibility of obtaining revenge on the Host.

COMMENT AND SUMMARY: Sir Hugh Evans has waited for Caius. Finally, he arrives in the company of the Host. They insult each other, but eventually make up their quarrel and swear joint revenge on the Host for the trick he has played upon them. This revenge motif is never developed in the rest of the play. The scene succeeds in showing up the cowardice of Sir Hugh Evans.

ACT III: SCENE 2

This scene takes place in the street early next morning. Mistress Page enters followed by Falstaff's page, Robin, and meets Ford, who is very suspicious of the lady's announced intention of visiting his wife. His distrust is strengthened when he discovers that Robin is Falstaff's page. In a few moments, Ford is joined by his companions, Page, Shallow, Slender, the Host, Sir Hugh, Doctor Caius, and Jack Rugby. In the meantime, the ladies have decided to play a trick on Falstaff. Shallow and Slender announce that they cannot stay to talk since they are about to dine with Anne Page to discuss a match between her and Slender. Doctor Caius then claims that Mistress Quickly has said that Anne is in love with him. But the Host proceeds to discuss the suit of Master Fenton with Page, who objects quite violently to the young man. Fenton, he says, has no money, he has been a companion of the "wild prince" Hal; he is of too high a social station and he is too clever to be suitable. In other words, Page will refuse his consent to Fenton.

COMMENT AND SUMMARY: This scene is largely a filler aimed at indicating the passage of time so that Mistress Ford and Mistress Page can get their plot in operation. It also shows that Fenton is unacceptable to Master Page as a suitor for Anne because of his penniless state and high social station.

ACT III: SCENE 3

This scene takes place inside the house of Master Ford. Mistress Ford and Mistress Page busily arrange for a basket of dirty washing to be placed in the room, repeating their orders of the previous day. When called for, the servants are to take the basket and empty it into the muddy ditch at Datchet-mead. Robin, the page, then announces the arrival of Sir John Falstaff. Mistress Page withdraws. Falstaff enters to embark on a high-flown bit of wooing Mistress Ford, complete with promises of marriage—if only Ford were dead. Mistress Ford accuses the knight of loving Mistress Page, which he denies. In the midst of this wooing, Mistress Page rushes in, gasping as if she has been running, to warn the "lovers" that Master Ford is approaching. Mistress Ford appears to think of the dirty clothes basket for the first time, and Falstaff readily squeezes himself inside to be carried past the unsuspecting Ford just as he arrives with Page, Caius, and Evans to search the house. Finding nothing suspicious, Ford takes his friends out to buy them the dinner he had promised if their mission were unsuccessful.

SUMMARY: This scene represents the first humbling of Falstaff. The knight, afraid of being found by Ford, hides himself in a laundry basket which the ladies have arranged to have emptied into a muddy ditch in Datchet-mead. Ford's attempt to prove his wife dishonest fails, and the merry wives decide to play another similar trick on Falstaff.

ACT III: SCENE 4

This scene takes places in a room in Page's house. Fenton and Anne, obviously in love, discuss Master Page's opposition to the young man's suit. He lists Page's opposition to him: his high social station, his need to marry money because of his debt-ridden estate, and his former wild habits. The major objection is, however, Page's belief that Fenton merely wishes to marry Anne because of her property. Anne says that her father may well be right, but Fenton denies it. Then, in an honest manner, he tells Anne that at first he had wooed her for her money, but that now he is love with her, not with her dowry.

> **COMMENT:**   Page's objections were justified. It was not uncommon for Elizabethan noblemen with empty purses to marry middle-class girls with the money to fill them. Love was not considered in these matches.

At this moment, Shallow, Slender, and Mistress Quickly arrive and we discover that Slender is Page's choice since he has three hundred pounds a year. Thus, we see another side of Page. Slender tries to woo, but he does not know what to say. Shallow promises a jointure of a hundred and fifty pounds, half the annual value of Slender's estate. But Slender does not truly care for Anne herself. He would just as readily woo another girl.

> **COMMENT:**   Both Shallow and Page are concerned with the financial aspects of the match, as well as the political contact with a Justice of the Peace. A "jointure" was the widow's share of her husband's estate. Page and his wife now enter, and Page acts as a strong-willed father who expects obedience from his daughter. He tells Anne to love Slender, and orders Fenton to be gone. As he

leaves, Fenton begs Mistress Page for her approval of his suit. In her turn, Anne begs her mother not to permit her marriage to Slender. Mistress Page then announces her candidate, Doctor Caius, a prospect which horrifies Anne. Nevertheless, Mistress Page seems kinder to Fenton than her husband, and she appears to offer him some hope. At the end of the scene, Mistress Quickly seems to think that Master Fenton is probably the most worthy of the three suitors from whom she has taken money.

COMMENT AND SUMMARY: Master Page, in trying to arrange the marriage of Anne for purely monetary considerations, was following a custom that was familiar to Elizabethan audiences. A wealthy girl of the middle, or upper, classes was not expected to marry for love. Indeed, it was generally believed that parents ought to have complete control over the marriage of their children because they were experienced and their judgment would not be corrupted by physical passion. This scene advances the plot of the marriage of Anne Page, showing that Slender is Page's choice, Doctor Caius that of Mistress Page, and Fenton has Anne, herself, as his champion.

ACT III: SCENE 5

This scene takes place in a room of the Garter Inn. Falstaff has just returned, wet through from his dumping, and angry due to his discomfiture. He calls Bardolph to bring him some sack (sherry), and, while he is waiting, Mistress Quickly brings him a message from Mistress Ford asking him to come to her between eight and nine the next morning. Falstaff agrees. He meets Ford, disguised as Brook, who has just arrived and pours out the tale of his being pushed into the laundry basket and dropped into the water to Brook. Then, after a few more insulting remarks about Master Ford, he says that he is to meet Mistress Ford again the next morning, between eight and nine. The scene concludes with Ford, left alone, making angry plans to catch Falstaff and his wife together.

COMMENT AND SUMMARY: This scene repeats what we already know about Falstaff's being carried out in the laundry basket and dropped in a muddy stream. This repetition adds humor to the play and arouses Ford's jealousy. It also sets up the second assignation between Mistress Ford and Falstaff and gives Ford another chance to catch his wife.

ACT IV: SCENE 1

This scene takes place in the street. Mistress Page and her son William meet Mistress Quickly. Mistress Page learns that Falstaff will keep the appointment and says that she will visit after she leaves William in school. Sir Hugh Evans enters and Mistress Page discovers that school has been dismissed for the day. A pleasantly amusing and irrelevant question-and-answer scene then takes place in which Sir Hugh quizzes William in his Latin and Mistress Quickly mistakes the meanings of the words causing confusion.

COMMENT AND SUMMARY: This scene seems rather disassociated from the rest of the play, but it does create amusement and is a satire on the educational methods of the day.

ACT IV: SCENE 2

This scene takes place in Ford's house a short time later. Falstaff interrupts his wooing of Mistress Ford to hide when Mistress Page arrives to warn her friend that Master Ford is coming to look for Sir John. She says it is lucky that he is not there. When Sir John hears this, he reveals himself but he refuses to get into the laundry basket again. Then, after a suspenseful display of puzzlement, Mistress Ford suggests dressing him in the gown of her maid's aunt, the Witch of Brentford—a very fat woman who has left an old gown upstairs. Falstaff readily agrees and leaves to don the dress.

Ford, Shallow, Caius, and Sir Hugh Evans appear and call for Mistress Ford. Her husband, in particular, accuses her of dishonesty, and spying the laundry basket, insists on searching it thoroughly. Of course, he finds nothing, but when he looks up, he sees what he thinks to be the woman he hates more than any other—the Witch of Brentford. Filled with rage, he reminds the "witch," who is, of course, Falstaff in disguise, that he had promised that he would beat her out of his house if she came to it again, and he starts to do so. After the unhappy Falstaff departs, the wives decide to tell their husbands of the tricks they have played on him.

COMMENT AND SUMMARY: This scene advances the plot of Falstaff's discomfiture, and also reveals both the jealously of Ford and the resourceful nature of the wives. Ford expected a repetition of the laundry basket trick; instead, the women sent Falstaff out disguised as the Witch of Brentford. Therefore Falstaff is beaten by Ford, who detests the fat woman because she is a conjurer.

ACT IV: SCENE 3

This short, and apparently unrelated scene, takes place in a room at the Garter Inn. Bardolph announces that the Germans desire three of the Host's horses because the Duke needs them. The Host offers some objection, but finally agrees and they all leave.

COMMENT AND SUMMARY: This scene is thought to be part of a joke at the expense of a German, Frederick of Württemberg, who tried for many years to be admitted to the Order of the Garter. Frederick was a knight-elect at the time the play was probably performed. [*See* Green, bibliography, for all comments on topic references.]

ACT IV: SCENE 4

This scene takes place in Ford's house. Page, Ford, Mistress Page, Mistress Ford, and Sir Hugh Evans are there. The wives obviously have told their husbands the jokes they have played on Falstaff, and Ford is repentant for his suspicion. Mistress Page suggests one last trick on the knight. They are to have Sir John come to Herne's Oak in Windsor Forest, wearing horns on his head to represent the ghost of Herne the Hunter which is said to haunt that particular tree. Anne Page, with a company of children, will pretend to be elves, fairies, and goblins. When they see Falstaff they will ask what such an unclean creature is doing there and will pinch him and burn him with their torches until he cries for mercy. Mistress Page announces that Anne will wear white. Master Page then decides that, since all these happenings will take place at night, he will have Slender steal Anne away and marry her secretly during the melee. Mistress Page, however, has the same idea, only she plans that Anne will be stolen away and secretly married to Doctor Caius; and further, she will make sure that Anne is dressed in green. Mistress Page's motives are not only to secure the doctor's money, but also to make use of his connections.

SUMMARY: This scene gets ready for the final trick on Falstaff, and the ultimate untangling of the plot.

1. Falstaff is to be disguised as Herne the Hunter with the cuckold's horns on his head—a fitting headgear for the man who wished to lure honest wives into unfaithfulness. He is to go to Herne's Oak in Windsor Forest at midnight.

2. Anne Page, as the Queen of the Fairies, will be there with a group of children trained by Sir Hugh Evans. When they see Falstaff they will pinch and burn him until he screams.

3. Master Page plans that Anne will steal away with Slender to be secretly married.

4. Mistress Page plans that Anne will steal away with Doctor Caius to be secretly married.

ACT IV: SCENE 5

This scene takes place in a room of the Garter Inn. The Host and Simple discuss Falstaff and the fat woman. Falstaff tells of his troubles in his disguise as the Witch of Brentford. At this point, Bardolph rushes in to say that the Germans have run off with the Host's horses. Caius also comes in to say the Duke de Jarmany is an imposter.

> **COMMENT:** There seems no relation between this incident and the rest of the scene. It is thought to be a slightly altered reference to an actual incident. The Duke de Jarmany may represent Frederick, Duke of Württemberg.

Mistress Quickly then appears and claims that Mistress Ford was beaten black and blue by her husband. Quickly also hints at further disclosures to come.

ACT IV: SCENE 6

In another room in the Garter Inn, Fenton is talking to the Host. He tells him about the intended confusions concerning Anne that are planned for that night, and asks that the Host arrange for a vicar to marry him to Anne between twelve and one in the morning. After initial reluctance, the Host agrees, especially when he is offered one hundred pounds for his trouble.

ACT V: SCENE 1

In a room in the Garter Inn, Mistress Quickly, who has given Mistress Ford's message to Falstaff, offers to get him a set of horns for the occasion. The fat knight is doubtful about trying his luck a third time, but he decides to go. Ford then appears, disguised as Brook, and Falstaff tells him about his beating and then says he is going to the forest.

ACT V: SCENE 2

In Windsor Forest, Page, Shallow, and Slender enter and discuss the way in which Slender is to recognize Anne. She will be in white, and when Slender cries "mum" she will cry "budget." Then they will run off to be married.

ACT V: SCENE 3

In a street leading to the park, Mistress Ford, Mistress Page, and Doctor Caius engage in a parallel scene to the preceding one. Mistress Page says that Anne will be in green and that she and the entire group of children are already hidden. They set off for Herne's Oak.

ACT V: SCENES 4-5

In Windsor Forest, Sir Hugh organizes his fairies and elves and cautions them to remember their roles.

In another part of the park, Falstaff enters disguised with horns as Herne the Hunter. In order to give himself courage, he recalls the various disguises of Jupiter when he wanted to gain a particular lady for himself. Mistress Ford then arrives with Mistress Page and calls for Falstaff as her deer. When Falstaff realizes that the two merry wives are there he speaks lovingly to both of them, suggesting that he be divided between them. A sudden noise is heard and the ladies run away.

Sir Hugh Evans, disguised, enters with Pistol as a hobgoblin. Mistress Quickly, Anne Page, and others follow with tapers. Falstaff, afraid, falls on his face. Mistress Quickly, as the Queen of the Fairies, calls her troops together, and Pistol delivers an elegant compliment to Queen Elizabeth by sending his forces to clean up the castle of Windsor: "Our radiant queen hates sluts and sluttery," or bad housekeeping of all kinds. Mistress Quickly then speaks of sending her fairies to Windsor Castle to polish the stalls of the members of the Order of the Garter in the Chapel, and also to sing the praises of the knights of the Order.

> **COMMENT:** This interpretation would seem to be correct in the light of most recent scholarship [*see* Green], particularly if, as seems likely, the play was first presented at a Garter celebration. The colors of green, purple, blue, and white that are mentioned are those of the Order.

The troops of fairies and elves then fall upon Falstaff, pinching him soundly. Doctor Caius is seen to lead off a boy dressed in green, while Slender steals off with a boy dressed in white. Fenton comes and steal off with the real Anne Page. Master Page, Mistress Page, and Mistress Ford then enter and Mistress Page reveals to Falstaff the extent of the trick they have played upon him. Ford also shows himself and laughs at the knight who realizes that the joke is on him. There is some raillery at the expense of Falstaff and also at Evans and his cheese-eating and Welsh background. The gaiety is interrupted by Slender who returns and announces that he was deceived by a boy dressed as he had been told Anne Page would be. He is followed by Doctor Caius who makes a similar complaint.

For the moment, no one present can decide who is with Anne Page. Then Fenton and his bride appear. In a speech which reproves both of Anne's parents for wishing to force her into a marriage of convenience, the bridegroom speaks of the love marriage they have just entered. This time, Master Ford rebukes Master Page. All ends happily, with a final ironic note that Master Brook "to-night shall lie with Mistress Ford."

SUMMARY: This entire act is composed of short scenes which bring about the final disentangling of the complicated plot.

1. Falstaff is disguised as Herne the Hunter, with appropriate headgear for the man who wants to cuckold husbands.

2. Master Page instructs Slender that he will recognize Anne, who will be dressed in white. Then he is to steal her away to marry her secretly.

3. Mistress Page instructs Doctor Caius that he will recognize Anne, who will be dressed in green. Then he is to steal her away to marry her secretly.

4. Sir Hugh Evans is disguised as the leader of the children and adults who are pretending to be fairies and elves. Mistress Quickly is disguised as the queen of the fairies.

5. Falstaff is burned with tapers and pinched as punishment.

6. All of the tricks which have been played on Falstaff are revealed by the Fords and the Pages.

7. Slender and Caius return, disgruntled, saying that they had stolen away boys who were dressed as they had been told Anne would be.

8. Master Fenton returns, accompanied by his bride, Anne Page and delivers a speech against forced marriages.

CHARACTER ANALYSES:
"THE MERRY WIVES OF WINDSOR"

On the whole the characters in this play are rather lightly drawn because the play depends for its amusement largely upon situation humor and the swiftness of its comic prose.

SIR JOHN FALSTAFF: Legend has it that this play was written because Queen Elizabeth wished to see Falstaff in love. Certainly, we have Falstaff in the throes of some kind of passion, but it can hardly be called "love." He is attracted to the ladies Ford and Page, but he is interested in them from either a physical or an economic point of view. Never does Falstaff feel anything like a grand passion. It is because of his determined assault on the chastity of the merry wives that Falstaff is punished, and his fate is well deserved. Perhaps, he has learned a lesson.

But the Falstaff of *The Merry Wives of Windsor* is by no means the same man who made life so merry in the history plays of Shakespeare. He has been taken out of his masculine environment and led to dance after ladies, a situation which does not suit him in the least. There are still some remnants of the old wit, but the play is best appreciated if we consider Falstaff as a character entirely divorced from his historical Shakespearean appearances. As a figure of comedy, a "trunk of humours," who receives the punishment he deserves, he is amusing; as the Falstaff of the history plays, he is not in his proper setting.

MISTRESS PAGE: She is a pleasant, merry, and resourceful middle-class woman who controls her own purse and who has had the good fortune to marry a man who respects her independence. It is she who initially thinks of revenge on Falstaff, and she never for a moment considers being disloyal to her husband. In the matter of Anne's marriage, we would today consider her wrong, but in the Elizabethan period she would have been considered fairly sensible. She wishes her daughter to marry a man with learning, money, and good connections at court. From the romantic view, she is, however, to be blamed for attempting to force her daughter into a loveless match.

MISTRESS FORD: She is the second merry wife, but she is, by no means, a copy of Mistress Page. Part of the reason for her different behavior is the fact that she is married to a husband who suspects her loyalty and, therefore, he tends to curb her independence. She is flattered by Falstaff's letter, but she is soon angry when she sees its duplicate in Mistress Page's possession. Nevertheless, she is a woman of honesty, spirit, and resourcefulness. She enters wholeheartedly into the game of teaching Falstaff, and, incidentally, her own husband, a lesson. At the end of the play, she has probably gained the trust of Master Ford.

MASTER FORD: He is the stock figure of the jealous husband, but he is unusually lucky in that his wife is not unfaithful to him, which is the usual fate for such a man. At the end of the play, he is given his own moment of moral superiority when he has lines which rebuke George Page and oppose marriage for money. "Wives are sold by fate," and as the play suggests, no man can change the course of true love.

MASTER PAGE: He is the precise opposite of Master Ford. Where Ford is jealous, Page is completely secure in his belief in the innocence and love of his wife. In this respect, the two men act as foils to each other. But Page has his weak spot when he reveals himself as a strict Elizabethan father who insists on his daughter's marrying for money rather than love. He looks after Anne's financial security very well, but her heart never enters into his consideration. To our emancipated modern eyes, therefore, it is completely just that Anne should disobey and deceive him in order to marry the man she loves. In marriage, however, the Pages seem to have an admirable relationship of mutual respect.

SIR HUGH EVANS AND DOCTOR CAIUS: These two characters are easily treated together because their comic nature arises largely from the way in which they mutilate the English language, the one with a Welsh, and the other with a French, accent. There are many jokes about Welsh-men in this play, but they are never bitter, and are often concerned with the Welshman's alleged liking for cheese. Both Evans, who supports Slender's suit to Mistress Anne, and Caius, who wants her for himself, are cowards, particularly, in the matter of their non-duel.

ANNE PAGE: She is very lightly drawn, but is a charming example of young womanhood who finally has enough courage to follow her heart and marry Fenton, despite her parents' wishes.

FENTON: He is a young gentleman who has led a merry and slightly lawless life. As a companion to Prince Hal, he has spent most of his in-heritance, but he is now eager to settle down. At first, as Fenton candidly admits, he had been interested in Anne because of the money she would bring with her, but later his interest is in Anne herself. Both he and Anne are young enough and sufficiently in love to forget the practicalities of an economically oriented marriage. As a result, they are married secretly, and take the risk of receiving nothing from Master Page because of Anne's defiance of him.

MISTRESS QUICKLY: She is a shrewd and witty operator, a woman who knows how to work for five different people, and several conflicting interests, simultaneously. She takes money from all of them and can turn almost any situation to her own personal advantage. She acts as go-between to Anne for all the suitors. She also participates in the plots against Falstaff by carrying notes from the merry wives to him.

ESSAY QUESTIONS FOR REVIEW:

1. What are the major attitudes towards love and marriage in this play? There are four distinct attitudes. The *first* is that of Sir John Falstaff, who is popularly supposed to be shown in love in *The Merry Wives of Windsor*. But Falstaff's love is lustful rather than romantic and it presupposes physical gratification rather than any intense intellectual or spiritual passion.

The *second* attitude is that which is shown by Master Ford in his treatment of his wife. He, like many other Elizabethans, seems to consider his wife "the weaker vessel"; therefore, he suspects Mistress Ford of infidelity merely on the accusation of Falstaff's disappointed rogues.

A *third* attitude, however, completely contradicts this one, because Master Page trusts his wife absolutely, and she does not abuse either his trust or his money.

Nevertheless, even the Pages are not perfect in their attitude (the *fourth*) towards love and marriage, because, although they trust each other, they do not wish to trust their daughter Anne's judgment. They take great pains to find a husband for her who will be advantageous in terms of money and position at court in the person of Dr. Caius (who is Mistress Page's candidate), or Slender, the Justice's cousin (who is Master Page's choice). Anne, however, chooses a young man, Fenton, for love alone and they elope. By the end of the play, all three sets of characters are brought to a new attitude concerning love and marriage. Ford repents his jealousy; the Pages see that they were wrong in trying to force Anne to marry a man she did not love; while Anne and Fenton stand for the virtue and honesty of true love in marriage.

2. What kinds of characters are portrayed in this play and how are they treated?

Like *The Comedy of Errors* this play is unusual in that it deals almost entirely with persons of the middle class. But here Shakespeare has dealt with English men and women. The only member of the nobility who is involved is Sir John Falstaff, and he is a man who hardly represents his social class in this play. The main characters, the Pages, the Fords, and Fenton, are all members of the merchant class, while such persons as Caius, Shallow, and Slender, are members of professions rather than persons of noble birth. Use is also made of dialect humor in the speech of Sir Hugh Evans, the Welsh schoolmaster, who may, indeed, have been a portrait of someone known at Elizabeth's court.

The language of this play is highly colloquial and most of the play is written in prose. The atmosphere and the situations found here are all typically English, Shakespeare seems to have observed the behavior of his characters very carefully.

Some of the characters are types: most notably, Master Ford, the jealous husband, a man who was usually a figure of fun in Elizabethan England. Falstaff, however, is a merry, roistering figure, and Dame Quickly has a life of her own. Fenton and Anne are fairly conventional lovers, while the Pages are typical Elizabethan parents judging by their manner of arranging Anne's marriage. The merry wives themselves achieve life and vigor through their imaginative trickery.

3. What is the structure of this play, and on what does its comedy depend?

The play evolves on two plots, the main action being the wooing of the merry wives by Sir John Falstaff, and the subplot, the love affair between Anne and Fenton, together with the procession of suitors for her hand. The two plots are tied together by the person of Dame Quickly who acts as go-between for the characters in both the main plot and the sub-plot. She carries messages for all the wooers of Mistress Anne, and is employed by Mistresses Ford and Page to bring messages to Falstaff, who, in turn, sends her to the ladies. At the end of the play, she takes part in the plot to discomfit Falstaff; indeed, she supplies him with the deer horns (the sign of a cuckold) for the last scene at Herne's Oak. She plays each person off against the other, but she does not really manipulate the action: the merry wives, Anne and Fenton control the two plots. However, Dame Quickly does make a profit.

The comic effect of this play depends entirely upon rapid action. At the same time, there is an underlying theme of crime and punishment. Falstaff, in attempting to prey upon the wives, must be punished, and as his fault is fleshly, so must he be punished by water, by beating, and then by fire. At the same time, the mercenary scheming of the Pages must prove unsuccessful, as, indeed, it does. Love and virtue must triumph and those characters who need to gain insight about themselves see the error of their ways.

ALL'S WELL THAT ENDS WELL

THE PLAY: This play is commonly called one of the "Dark Comedies," or "Problem Comedies," because the action seems to be more tragic rather than comic. In fact, about *the only reason* that *All's Well* can be called a "comedy" is that it ends happily for the central characters. It is a play which seems to be lacking in feeling, even as related to the two main characters. Bertram's action in deserting Helena is unpleasant, and Helena's resourcefulness in fulfilling her assigned tasks tends, oddly enough, to alienate sympathy from her. By the time this comedy was written, probably 1602-03, Shakespeare had entered his tragic period, and his comic gift seems to have been temporarily submerged. Feeling and humor seem to be subordinated to a highly logical, even legalistic, approach to the relationships between men and women. This play is also the first occasion in which Shakespeare makes use of the "bed-trick," the substitution of one woman for another in bed in order to deceive a lover. Many critics have thought that such a trick ruins the character of Helena, but, actually, she is simply trying to obtain her matrimonial rights, and is by no means immoral. She is honest enough to know what she wants, and to go after it.

SOURCE AND TEXT: The source of the play is Boccaccio's tale of Giletta de Nerbona in the *Decameron*. It was translated into English by William Paynter in his volume, *The Palace of Pleasure* (1566). Boccaccio's *novella* (a tale longer than a short story and shorter than a novel) was itself derived from medieval folk literature. Shakespeare follows his source fairly closely, although he does invent the characters of Parolles, the flatterer and braggart, the Countess, Lafeu, and the Clown.

The play was first published in the First Folio of 1623 and the text is considered satisfactory. The frequent shifting from verse to prose is notable. In general, the comic characters, such as the Clown and Parolles, speak in prose, while the nobler persons speak poetry. Nevertheless, the Countess has a considerable number of prose lines.

THE PLOT: The play opens with a sad scene. Bertram, son of the late Count of Roussillon, is leaving his mother to go with his companion, the evil-minded Parolles, to the court of France. He is now under the guardianship of the King, who has for a time been ill with an ulcer. But Bertram and the Countess of Roussillon are not the only ones who feel sad. Helena, the daughter of the late physician to the Roussillon family, who has been brought up like a sister to Bertram, must remain. She is finally brought to admit her love for Bertram to the Countess; she tells her that she has decided to follow Bertram to the French court in an attempt to cure the King of his complaint, using one of her father's prescriptions. The Countess gently encourages her.

When Helena arrives at court, the King of France does not fully trust her skill, despite his knowledge of her father's reputation. She then makes a bargain with him: she will pledge her life that she can help him, and, if she is successful, she asks only that she be allowed to choose her own husband from the ranks of the eligible nobles of the court. Helena's cure is successful, and when she is given her choice, she, of course, chooses Bertram. Other lords would have been glad to gain her hand, but not Bertram. He objects to the low social status of Helena. Nevertheless, the King, as Bertram's guardian, insists that his ward accept Helena, so the marriage is performed.

But Bertram is not yet beaten. He runs away to the wars in Tuscany and sends Helena a letter telling her that, until she can obtain his ancestral ring from his finger, and have a child begotten by him, then and then only will he accept her as his wife—certainly, an impossible task, one would think.

Helena, who has been at Roussillon, then sets off as a pilgrim. She arrives in Florence where she hears stories of the valor of Bertram and also of the licentious way in which Parolles leads his master into evil ways. A widow, who invites Helena to lodge at her house, tells how Bertram has been soliciting her own daughter, Diana, to be his mistress. Helena at this point has a plan and suggests that things be so arranged that Diana pretend to agree to Bertram's request, but Helena will herself take Diana's place in bed in order to fulfill her husband's conditions. The Widow agrees, and Helena also has Diana obtain Bertram's ring before she agrees to the appointment. She tells the girl to promise that the ring will be replaced by another when they are in bed together.

Everything goes according to plan. Afterwards, when Bertram returns to the camp he finds that his braggart-soldier friend, Parolles, is to be tested for his courage. Of course, he turns out to be an utter coward.

Helena, Diana, and the Widow all return to France where they go to the court. In the meantime, Bertram has also returned, and believes, in common with everyone else, that Helena is dead. As a result, he now begins to appreciate her virtue. He is in the process of contracting a marriage to another woman when he is asked to give a ring to her father as a betrothal token. He gives the ring that "Diana" had given him in bed. The King immediately recognizes it as one that he himself had given to Helena. The King asks how Bertram obtained it, and when the young man lies frantically, he accuses him of having killed Helena. At this moment, a letter from Diana is brought in. She calls for justice since Bertram has not kept his promise to marry her. She then enters and tells her story, supported by her mother. Bertram tries to wriggle out of his difficulty and is saved only by the appearance of Helena who announces the fulfillment of all his conditions. Bertram now willingly accepts his wife, Diana is offered a large dowry and the promise of suitable husband, and *All's Well That Ends Well.*

DETAILED SUMMARY OF "ALL'S WELL THAT ENDS WELL"

ACT I: SCENE 1

The play opens in the palace of the Count of Roussillon with the entry of the Countess of Roussillon with her son; Bertram, Lafeu, a French Lord; and Helena, the daughter of the recently deceased family physician. The company are wearing black and are in mourning for the late Count. There is added sadness too, because Bertram is about to leave home for the court of the King of France. His presence has been commanded there since, with the death of his father, he is now the ward of the King.

COMMENT: This custom of wardship was a development of the feudal relationship between vassal and lord, but in England it had been revived as a money-making project for the monarch. It meant that the King became the guardian of the child of a deceased vassal, and, in effect, the administrator of his lands and person. The guardian also had the right to arrange the marriage of his ward, but only to someone of equal rank—a stipulation that the King ignores later in this play.

In the course of conversation, the health of the King of France is discussed and we find that he is seriously ill. The Countess comments that the late Gerard de Narbon might have been able to cure the King of his ailment, an ulcerous sore. Helena is then identified as the daughter of this recently deceased physician. The Countess has kindly kept the girl in her own house which is the only home she has ever known.

Suddenly, the Countess notes that Helena is again weeping, and she chides her for it. Bertram and Lefeu bid farewell and leave. Then we learn that Helena's grief is not for her dead father, but because of the departure of Bertram. She is in love with this young man whose appearance charms her, but her reason tells her that he is far above her social station. She, a mere doctor's daughter, cannot hope to marry a count and a ward of the King.

Parolles, a follower of Bertram then enters. He is "a notorious liar, . . . a great way fool, solely a coward," according to Helena, who nevertheless treats him well for the sake of his master. He engages in a bawdy conversation on the subject of virginity, a state of which he disapproves. Then he leaves to follow Bertram to the court. When Helena is alone, she delivers a soliloquy, revealing her inmost thoughts and hinting at a plan that concerns her curing the King's disease.

SUMMARY: This opening scene serves important functions by introducing us to the basic relationships in the play and to the main characters.

1. Bertram is the hero. His father has died recently and he, himself, has just been called to the court of his guardian, the King of France.

2. Helena, the heroine, is desperately in love with Bertram. She, however, as a physician's daughter, is inferior to him in social rank.

3. The Countess of Roussillon has taken Helena into her own house and is kind and affectionate to the orphan.

4. Lafeu, a pleasant, kind French Lord, knows about the illness of the King of France.

5. Parolles follows Bertram to court. He is a bawdy, rather cowardly man. But, since Bertram likes him for his merriment, Helena speaks with him.

ACT 1: SCENE 2

This scene takes place after a lapse long enough for Bertram to travel from Roussillon to Paris. The King enters with his attendants and begins to discuss the wars in Tuscany between Siena and Florence in which France may yet become involved. Bertram then appears to be greeted warmly by the King who praises the virtues and abilities of his father, the late Count. At the same time, the King draws attention to his own physical infirmity and regrets the death of Gerard de Narbon who, he is certain, would have been able to help him.

SUMMARY: This scene acts as a bridge to further separate actions. It shows Bertram's position at court and introduces the illness of the King again. The skill of Helena's late father is praised. In this way, the scene is tied to the preceding one.

ACT I: SCENE 3

This scene takes place at the palace at Roussillon. The Countess and the Steward try to discuss Helena, but the Clown interrupts and speaks merrily about his own desire to marry, simply for physical necessity, despite his belief that his wife will probably be unfaithful to him. The Steward finally does speak; he tells the Countess of Helena's love for Bertram, but makes it clear that the young lady considers Bertram far beyond her reach. The Countess sends for Helena and then sympathetically remembers the sorrows of her own youth. With the arrival of Helena, the Countess finally coerces her to admit her love for Bertram. Upon further questioning, the girl says that she has intended to go to the French court herself, for the purpose of alleviating the King's illness with her father's medicines. When the Countess raises the objection that the court physicians will hardly listen to a young girl, Helena declares herself willing to risk her life in the attempt. The Countess cheerfully and lovingly gives her permission to go to Paris.

SUMMARY: This scene has three aspects:

1. The Clown speaks of marriage and the relationship between the sexes on a physical level only. This area of bawdiness, the province of Parolles, operates as a contrast to the pure love Helena has for Bertram.

2. The loving relationship between the Countess and Helena is established. This affection will later alienate Bertram from the audience.

3. It gives the reason for Helena's journey to Paris and foreshadows her plan.

ACT II: SCENE 1

We are again in Paris, and the King enters with Bertram and Parolles. The young Lords are about to leave for the Florentine wars. After wishing them well, he retires. Bertram, left alone with Parolles, is chafing impatiently at being left behind because of his youth, while Parolles boasts loudly of his military experience. They then leave. The King enters to greet Lafeu who says that he has seen a medicine which will cure the monarch's illness. To the King's surprise, the new physician is a young woman, but he agrees to receive her. Helena then identifies herself and explains how she inherited a prescription for the King's complaint from her father, Gerard de Narbon. Needless to say, the monarch is doubtful of her skill, but Helena gambles her life that she will succeed in a cure within two days. If she fails, she will be executed, but, if she succeeds, she asks that she be permitted to choose a husband from among the lords of the royal court, not a man of royal blood, but someone whom the king commands.

COMMENT AND SUMMARY: This scene reveals the behavior of Bertram and Parolles at court. Bertram is probably under twenty, and he is still immature. The scene also advances the plot by having Helena persuade the King to place himself under her care. She will be executed if she fails in her cure, but given the free choice of a husband from among the French lords if she succeeds. Helena's powers of persuasion are shown here clearly.

ACT II: SCENE 2

The action returns to Roussillon where the Fool is amusing the Countess who suddenly remembers the real business of the interview and gives him a letter for Helena.

COMMENT AND SUMMARY: This short scene is a dramatic device to indicate the passage of time. The Clown is established as the professional fool of the Roussillon household.

ACT II: SCENE 3

In Paris, in the palace of the King, Bertram, Lafeu, and Parolles are discussing the almost miraculous cure of the monarch. Apparently, Helena has been successful. Lafeu and Parolles retire. The King, Helena, and various attendants enter. In accordance with the bargain made with the King, Helena proceeds to choose a husband from among the lords of France. She begins her suit by stating her virtue; her beauty speaks for itself. Of the first four lords she addresses, not one would refuse her suit. Then she comes to Bertram and she *gives* herself to him.

> **COMMENT:** Helena is extremely humble here. She feels unworthy to use the common form of words for an engagement to marry, "I *take* thee."

Bertram is angered at being singled out thus. He asks permission to choose his own wife—a quite reasonable request. He does not see why he must be sacrificed for the King's cure. He quite frantically seeks for a way out of the situation by complaining that Helena is not noble enough to marry him: "A poor physician's daughter my wife!"

> **COMMENT:** Despite our current views on social status, a physician in the sixteenth century was considered as merely a superior trades-man, unless, of course, he was of noble birth.

The King counters Bertram's argument by saying that Helena is virtuous, "young, wise, fair," and in those respects she is noble. Anyway, he will ennoble her with a title and a dowry, if that is what Bertram wants.

> **COMMENT:** Every bride was expected to bring money to her marriage as a *dowry* which would be returned to her if she were widowed. In return, a husband was expected to arrange a *jointure*, a share in his estate if he died first. Note that here the King is, in effect, violating the rules of guardianship in forcing Bertram to marry beneath his rank. The purpose of this situation is to gain some sympathy for Bertram. His objections are justified; however, he is the only lord of the court who refuses Helena.

Finally, the King loses his temper and enforces his authority. He makes Bertram take Helena's hand and repeat the words of betrothal. The actual marriage will take place later in the evening. Left alone, Lafeu and Parolles discuss the affair, and the old Lord says that Bertram was wise to obey the King. Parolles hotheadedly disagrees. Lafeu leaves, to return a short time later to announce that the young people are now married. His second departure is followed by the arrival of the irate Bertram who swears that he will rush away to the Tuscan wars to avoid going to bed with Helena.

> **COMMENT:** Bertram's decision is astute. He might be able to annul the marriage contract on a technicality if he does not bed Helena.

SUMMARY: This scene sets up the action for the second portion of the play.

1. Helena has cured the King and she chooses Bertram as a husband in fulfillment of her bargain.

2. Bertram is unwilling to marry Helena. He does have some justification

in objecting since the King is forcing him to marry a girl of inferior rank and fortune to satisfy a debt of honor that is not even his.

3. The first part of the play is now concluded. Helena has achieved her marriage to Bertram. She must now gain physical possession of him.

ACT II: SCENES 4-5

The first scene takes place in a room of the King's palace in Paris. Helena is exchanging witicisms with the Countess's Clown when Parolles enters. He tells Helena that Bertram is forced to leave immediately on urgent business; therefore, he will not be able to consummate his marriage until later. He sends Helena a message asking her to make his excuses to the King.

In the next scene, also in the palace, Lafeu and Bertram discuss Parolles as a soldier. Bertram thinks him brave, but Lafeu is skeptical. Parolles, himself, arrives to say that all the preparations for departure have been made. Helena comes in with the King's permission for Bertram to leave. The young man says that he will be back in two days and tells Helena to do whatever she thinks fit. She humbly says farewell to her lord who, after her exit, says that he intends to keep far away from her.

COMMENT AND SUMMARY: These scenes in which Bertram decides to leave France rather than consummate his marriage to Helena are important in advancing the plot. The comments on the valor of Parolles point forward to the later disclosure of his cowardice. Bertram's friendship and respect for Parolles indicate his immaturity.

ACT III: SCENE 1

This short scene takes place in Florence at the palace of the Duke who is discussing the Tuscan wars with two French lords. The Duke is disappointed that France does not seek involvement. Nevertheless, one of the lords indicates that some of the more hotheaded youths of the French court will be willing to fight.

ACT III: SCENE 2

In Rousillon, the Countess indicates her happiness about her son's marriage to Helena. Bertram, however, has sent the Clown with a letter indicating that he has run away rather than go to bed with Helena. Regretfully, the Countess blames Bertram for his action, both for love of Helena and from the fear of vengeance by the King. Helena then enters with two gentlemen to tell the Countess that Bertram has gone away forever. She shows the Countess a letter in which Bertram sets her a series of impossible tasks: "When thou canst get the ring upon my finger which never shall come off, and show me a child begotten of my body that I am father to, then call me husband." So Bertram vows that he will not recognize Helena as his wife until she accomplishes these tasks, and predicts that she never will.

COMMENT: This part of the play has elements of the folklore of the "clever wench." An impossible condition is set and the woman fulfills it and gains her lover. The quality of Helena's character tends to be divided as a result of this tradition.

Helena, in her sadness, decides to steal away, so that Bertram may return to his home in Roussillon.

SUMMARY: This scene makes some very important points:

1. It establishes the Countess of Roussillon as friendly to Helena. She thinks Bertram is at fault for avoiding his marital duties.

2. It stipulates the conditions under which Bertram will accept Helena as his wife, and states his reluctance to do so.

3. It motivates Helena's flight to Florence, a repetition of the journey to Paris.

4. It gives Helena an additional characteristic, the resourcefulness of the "clever wench" of folklore.

ACT III: SCENE 3

This brief scene in Florence with the Duke, Bertram, Parolles, and assorted soldiers, serves to indicate the valor of Bertram and the favor in which Florence holds him. He undertakes danger boldly because he despises love.

ACT III: SCENE 4

Again in Roussillon, the Countess has just received Helena's farewell letter. The deserted wife says that she has gone away disguised as a pilgrim of St. Jacques—a common disguise for lovers. Helena tells the Countess that she may tell her son that Roussillon is free for him since she has left. The Countess is sad at Helena's departure and blames Bertram all the more. She tells her steward to write to Bertram emphasizing Helena's virtue and telling him of her departure in the hope that he will return home.

COMMENT AND SUMMARY: These two scenes are used solely for advancing the plot and are primarily expository. Scene 3 indicates the valorous conduct of Bertram, and Scene 4 shows the love and sorrow of Helena. The fact that the Countess blames Bertram rather than Helena reinforces our sympathy for the deserted wife.

ACT III: SCENE 5

This scene takes place outside the walls of Florence. An old widow enters with three young girls—Diana, Violenta, and Mariana—and other citizens. They have come to watch the soldiers return to the city. The valor of "the French Count" is praised, but Mariana warns Diana against that same Count who is soliciting her love. She further warns her about the immoral companion of that same Count. We then realize that we have found Bertram and Parolles.

At this point, Helena, dressed as a pilgrim to the shrine of St. Jacques le Grand, enters, and the Widow offers her and four or five other pilgrims lodging at her own house. Helena, in listening to the conversation hears the story of Bertram's marriage and the coarse report that Parolles has given of her. Diana expresses sympathy for the injured lady, and the Widow remarks that Diana could, indeed, do her a service. Upon Helena's questioning, the Widow reveals that Bertram is soliciting Diana's company for immoral purposes. Just then, the procession passes by and Helena sees her husband again. Diana praises Bertram, but makes cutting comments about Parolles.

SUMMARY: This scene is important because it not only advances the plot but reveals character development as well.

1. It shows the valor of Bertram. He has good qualities, but he is immature.

2. It reveals the way in which Parolles leads Bertram from virtue. Bertram's eyes must be opened somehow to this bad influence.

3. It introduces Diana, whom Parolles is soliciting for Bertram. She is honest and sympathetic to the cause of Helena.

4. It places Helena in Florence so that she is near Bertram.

5. It makes use of coincidence so that Helena immediately meets the Widow, the one person in Florence who can help her.

6. Some hints are given that the consummation of the marriage of Helena and Bertram is going to take place.

ACT III: SCENE 6

This scene takes place in the camp before Florence. Bertram speaks to two French lords who want to test the valor of Parolles. They plan to capture him and make him think that he is in the enemy camp. Then, if his behavior is as cowardly as the lords expect, Bertram may punish him. The lords suggest that Parolles be sent to fetch a drum that has been captured, since he has been boasting of a stratagem to get it back. Finally, Parolles says that he will undertake the mission. The scene concludes with Bertram taking a friend to show him the house in which the honest Diana lives.

COMMENT AND SUMMARY: This apparently unimportant material concerning the unmasking of Parolles as a coward serves a noteworthy purpose in the play. It opens the eyes of Bertram to the foolishness of his companion and brings him closer to a more mature appreciation of himself and of others.

ACT III: SCENE 7

This scene takes place in the house of the Widow in Florence. Helena has identified herself and tries to persuade the goodhearted Widow to help her. Helena's plan is that Diana should make an appointment to meet Count Bertram as he wishes, but, before she agrees, she should ask him for his ancestral ring. Then she should make an appointment to meet him in her bedchamber, when she will give Bertram another ring. But Diana herself will be absent, as Helena will take her place. In return, Helena promises to provide Diana with a large dowry. The Widow agrees to this plan.

> **COMMENT:** Some critics and readers have objected to this "bed-trick" as being beneath Helena, but, if one considers her in the "clever wench" tradition, acceptance is easier. Further, Helena is legally married to Bertram and she is merely trying to obtain her rights as a wife.

SUMMARY: This scene is the most important in the play for advancing the plot.

1. Helena plans to have Diana agree to Bertram's immoral proposition, but only after she gets the ring "which never shall come off."

2. Helena will take Diana's place in bed, and, in this manner, her marriage will be consummated. She will give Bertram another ring, the significance of which is revealed later.

ACT IV: SCENE 1

This scene takes place outside the Florentine camp. One of the French lords and five or six soldiers lie in ambush for Parolles to arrive in an attempt to recover a captured drum. When Parolles arrives, he simply goes through the motions of retrieving it. Finally, the soldiers seize and blindfold him, giving him the impression that he is in the hands of the enemy. Immediately, Parolles calls for mercy and offers to expose the secrets of the Florentine camp in exchange for his life.

COMMENT AND SUMMARY: This scene is used to separate the two episodes which take place in the house of the Widow. Shakespeare alternates the two parts of the plot in order to signify the passage of time. The scene also reveals the cowardice of Parolles.

ACT IV: SCENE 2

This scene takes place in the Widow's house in Florence and it concerns the wooing of Diana by Bertram. Helena's plot works out well. Diana is coyly reluctant and continually reminds Bertram of his duty to his wife. She obtains his ancestral ring after his initial reluctance to give it to her is overcome. He swears love for Diana; she makes an assignation with him. He is to come to her chamber window at midnight, but Diana imposes a further condition. Bertram must remain in her bed only one hour, and he must not speak to her. She, during that time, will put a ring on his finger as a token of her love.

> **COMMENT:** This exchange of rings is not clearly motivated here, but is for the purpose of identification in the last act; furthermore, the exchange of rings was a common outward symbol of betrothal.

Left alone, Diana is amazed at the deception of mankind. Bertram has promised to marry her after the death of his wife, but Diana is so disillusioned that she swears to die a maiden.

SUMMARY: This scene is concerned with the details of the "bed-trick" and, therefore, advances the plot.

1. Bertram's specious avowals of love indicate that his interest in Diana is physical, not spiritual.

2. Diana manages to obtain Bertram's ring "that never shall come off."

3. The assignation is made and the arrangements that make the substitution possible are clarified.

4. A further exchange of rings is arranged which will be important at the end of the play.

ACT IV: SCENE 3

We return to the Florentine camp where two French lords are discussing Bertram's matrimonial difficulties. The Countess's letter has arrived and it has apparently angered the young man. The lords agree that Bertram has deserved the displeasure of the King and the general blame he has incurred for his treatment of Helena. They mention also his assignation with Diana and say that they expect Bertram back in time to observe the exposure of Parolles' cowardice. There is a report that Helena is dead. Bertram appears, well satisfied with the report of Helena's death and with his night's amusement with the supposed Diana.

Parolles is then brought in and, when threatened with torture, he gives away vital information about the Florentine camp. He tells of troop strength, and also retails scandalous information about a particular nobleman. Finally, he makes insulting remarks about Bertram himself and is shown to have written a poem to Diana in which he calls the young man a fool. Bertram is astonished. Then Parolles calls for mercy. He is released for everyone to laugh him out of countenance.

COMMENT AND SUMMARY: This unmasking of the treacherous character Parolles, the braggart soldier, has a long history beginning with classical drama. Shakespeare here uses the device for two purposes. He sustains suspense about the developments in Florence, and further, he uses this incident to open Bertram's eyes to his own folly in accepting Parolles at his face value.

ACT IV: SCENE 4

We are again at the Widow's house where Helena rejoices over the success of her plan. She is about to set off for the French court, which is, at present, in Marseilles. Helena asks Diana to help her a bit more, and Diana agrees.

COMMENT AND SUMMARY: This scene, in which Helena decides to set off for Marseilles taking Diana and the Widow with her, is purely for purposes of furthering the plot.

ACT IV: SCENE 5

At Roussillon, Lafeu tells the Countess what has happened to Bertram since his departure. He recounts the way in which the young man was misled by Parolles and repeats the report of Helena's death. The Countess grieves for "the death of the most virtuous gentlewoman that nature had praise for creating," and regrets that she had ever known her own son. Lafeu then tells the Countess that, since he has heard of the death of Helena, he has spoken to the King concerning a match between his own daughter and Bertram. The Countess has no objections to this. The Clown has been trying to amuse everyone throughout the scene.

COMMENT AND SUMMARY: This scene is expository and conveys to the Countess information concerning the discomfiture of her son and the reported death of Helena. Lafeu's decision that his own daughter should marry Bertram indicates that the cynical and kindly lord believes that the young man has learned a lesson and has presumably grown up.

ACT V: SCENE 1

Helena, the Widow, and Diana have all arrived at Marseilles, only to find that the court has moved to Roussillon. Helena takes the opportunity of giving a gentleman who is traveling there a letter containing a petition to the King.

ACT V: SCENE 2

In front of the Count's palace in Roussillon, Parolles tries desperately to restore himself to favor with Lafeu, who sends him away with harsh words.

ACT V: SCENE 3

We are now inside the place at Roussillon, and the King, accompanied by the Countess, Lafeu, the two French lords, and various attendants enter. The King regrets the death of Helena and blames Bertram for not valuing her true worth. The Countess agrees; then Lafeu broaches the subject of a match between his daughter, Maudlin, and Bertram. The young man arrives and the King asks if he will consider the marriage. Bertram first expresses his sorrow for Helena's death, saying that he now perceives the true value of his dead wife, whom he had come to love. He agrees to marry Maudlin. The King asks for a token of love to send to the girl. Obedient to the King this time, Bertram draws a ring from his finger and gives it to Lafeu who says, with amazement, that he had seen it on Helena's finger when she was last at court. The King then looks at it and says that he, himself, had given it to Helena with instructions to send it to him if ever she needed his help.

The King and Lafeu both want more information about the ring and Bertram lies valiantly, claiming that it had been thrown to him from a window in Florence. The King, however, is unconvinced and suspects that Bertram has done away with his unloved wife. He orders the arrest of the young man, and as he is carried away, Bertram says that it is as easy to prove the ring Helena's as to prove that he had been to bed with Helena in Florence. He does not know the irony of his comment.

At this moment, a letter is brought in signed Diana Capilet, which accuses Bertram of leaving Florence without having fulfilled his promise to marry her after the death of his wife, although he had been to bed with her on the strength of that promise. Diana has now come to request the King that he require Bertram to keep his vow. Bertram is brought back to the presence of the King and he desperately tries to deny everything.

Diana, who is now present, claims him as her husband and produces his ancestral ring as evidence of his vow. She also calls a witness—Parolles. Almost babbling with fear, Bertram tries to give the impression that Diana had seduced him. But Diana then asks for "her" ring, which was the one that Lafeu and the King had recognized. Bertram then decides that it is best to tell the truth. Parolles gives his confusing evidence, and Diana tries, in riddling terms, to prove that she is Bertram's wife—in fact, if not in name. The King then tries to force Diana to say how she obtained the ring, but she so angers the King with pert answers that he threatens her with prison. In reply, Diana says that she will give bail, and sends her mother to get it.

Then Helena walks into the midst of all this confusion. She tells Bertram and the assembled company that she has fulfilled the conditions laid down in Bertram's letter: she has obtained his ring, and she is now with child by him. Then, humbly, she asks "Will you be mine, now you are doubly won?"

> COMMENT: The double winning is, of course, first, the actual wedding ceremony which made them legally man and wife, and second, the winning by Helena's fulfilling of Bertram's conditions.

Bertram, who had almost had to enter a contract to marry Diana, agrees joyfully to Helena's plea. Nevertheless, he is still puzzled over some details. The King, himself, a trifle confused, then says that if Diana is a maiden, as she claims, he will give her a large dowry and she may choose a husband for herself. And so *"All's Well That Ends Well."*

SUMMARY: Shakespeare makes much use of coincidence in untangling this plot.

1. The King leaves Marseilles and goes to Roussillon to stay with the widowed Countess.

2. Helena, Diana, and the Widow arrive in time for everyone to meet at Roussillon.

3. Bertram returns to court and his home at this time.

4. Lafeu recognizes Helena's ring. This kind of recognition by tangible, and extraneous, objects, is a common device for identification.

5. The Countess recognizes Bertram's ring in the possession of Diana.

6. Parolles just happens to be there to confirm Diana's story.

7. Bertram plays right into Helena's hands by his frantic lying to the King and the company.

8. Bertram repents of his former cruelty to Helena. He is also more obedient to the authority of the King. He has now matured and is worthy of Helena. By the end of the play he should also be thanking Helena for rescuing him from an unwanted match.

CHARACTER ANALYSES: "ALL'S WELL THAT ENDS WELL"

BERTRAM: He is one of Shakespeare's most unsympathetic heroes which is the main reason that this play has never been particularly popular. What exasperates the audience most about him is his blindness in not seeing Helena for the noble girl that she is. It must not be forgotten, however, that he is very young. He is still in wardship, and he is considered under age for the Tuscan wars, so we must consider him as somewhere between eighteen and twenty. Many of his character traits revealed by such things as his rash friendship with Parolles, must, therefore, be considered the result of immaturity. He must grow up, he must pass tests of valor, and he must understand himself before he will be worthy of Helena.

Nevertheless, Bertram does have some justification in refusing to wed Helena. The King of France is going beyond his powers as a guardian in forcing Bertram to marry a girl who is his social inferior. But, at the same time that the King's refusal to allow Bertram to speak for himself arouses our sympathy, the fact that all the other lords would have gladly accepted Helena quells it and arouses our displeasure. By the end of the play, Bertram has learned his lesson and will love Helena "dearly, ever, ever dearly."

HELENA: She is the only character in the play other than Bertram who is fully drawn. She is unusual in that she is a strong-minded, interesting good character, but not meek or dull. As a character, she seems to possess two sides. She is lovesick and determined to marry Bertram; yet, she is humble in her approach and admits his social superiority.

After her marriage, however, she becomes, in some respects, a stock character, the "clever wench" of folklore. Nevertheless, she retains a great deal of her own individuality. She, too, must prove herself resourceful and noble in behavior in order to raise herself to Bertram's social level and to be a worthy wife to him. Some critics comment that she lacks pride, and that she is a trifle shrewish in chasing after a man who does not want her, but she is still a virtuous girl who wishes to marry honorably, and, at the same time, to follow the call of her own heart.

THE COUNTESS OF ROUSSILLON: She is the "understanding older woman" of the play. On the whole, she is not fully developed as a character, but her understanding of Helena and her condemnation of her own son make his conduct seem reprehensible.

DIANA: She is a puzzle. At first, she seems to be a quiet, honest maiden and she gladly helps the wronged Helena achieve justice. But, in the last act of the play, she shows herself capable of pert answers and exasperating behavior that almost seem out of character, unless she is adopting a false attitude in order to frighten Bertram.

THE WIDOW: Diana's mother is an honest, kindly, moral woman who is glad to help Helena as long as her daughter's honor is not sacrificed.

PAROLLES: He is a development of the stock character of the braggart soldier who is eventually exposed. He is a merry, bawdy, rather unlikable, person who leads Bertram into evil. His punishment is well deserved, and he is useful as a means of displaying the growing maturity of Bertram.

LAFEU: He is the cynical, worldly-wise, and kindly French Lord who is the friend of both Helena and the Countess. At the end of the play, he seems to consider Bertram repentant enough to consider his marrying his own daughter, which indicates the extent of the change in the young man.

THE KING OF FRANCE: He is a man of his word, but he is also short-tempered and dislikes to be crossed by such a young man as Bertram. Diana also tries his patience greatly. He went beyond his powers as a guardian in forcing the unwilling Bertram to marry Helena.

ESSAY QUESTIONS FOR REVIEW: "ALL'S WELL THAT ENDS WELL"

1. What are the major themes of this play and how are they treated?

The major themes of *All's Well That Ends Well* are two: the triumph of love, and the maturing of a young man. In the first theme, we see Helena's attempts to gain possession of her husband. She is, indeed, very resourceful in the way she manages to fulfill Bertram's stipulations. But Helena is not content with merely gaining Bertram's person; she must also gain his love. She manages to do this through her plotting with Diana to have that young lady appear at the French court and accuse Bertram of dishonest behavior with her. Similarly, through the report of her death, Bertram begins to understand the virtue and the value of the lady whom he thinks he has lost. But Diana's behavior before the King makes Bertram doubly glad when Helena appears, because her virtuous, mild, gentle demeanor acts as a sharp contrast to Diana's pert answers.

The second theme concerns the awakening of Bertram's moral sense, as well as his love for Helena. His friendship with the evil-minded Parolles indicates that Bertram is a rather immature young man who cannot readily distinguish between virtue and vice. For this reason, he objects strenuously to his marriage with the virtuous Helena, because she is not of noble birth. He wants to be free to follow his desires, which he attempts when he goes to the wars in Tuscany. The unmasking of Parolles is, in many ways, a turning point in the development of Bertram. He realizes for the first time that his companion has been lying, making him look foolish, and leading him into evil ways.

Diana's arrival at court and her disclosure of his dishonesty makes him look even more foolish when he attempts to lie his way out of trouble. When Helena arrives, his pride is controlled and he is glad to settle down with the honest lady whom he once scorned, but who has believed in him steadfastly. He is now capable of recognizing that his once-despised wife is superior to him in that virtue which constitutes the truest nobility.

2. What constitutes *nobility* in this play?

Debate on the definition of *nobility* was common in the Renaissance. The discussion centered on whether nobility resided in birth, riches, or virtue. Bertram, it will be remembered, claimed that Helena lacked nobility of birth, but the King defines nobility in different terms. He claims that Helena possesses the gifts of natural virtue which, in effect, make her noble in a moral sense. As for the adjuncts of wealth and title, the King says that these can be more easily supplied than virtue.

On the other hand, Bertram possesses nobility of birth and wealth, but he does not yet possess the true nobility of virtue. Even if a young man were descended from a long line of noble ancestors, he would still not be considered truly noble until he had confirmed his birth and lineage by means of virtuous actions. By the end of the play, Bertram sees his error, and he understands that Helena is a lady who is worthy of him, and, in fact, superior to him. Her nobility is confirmed by her love and her virtuous belief in her wandering husband.

3. This play is often called a "dark comedy." What do you understand by this term? *Illustrate with specific reference to the play.*

The term "dark comedy," or sometimes "problem comedy," is used to describe two plays (and, sometimes, *Troilus and Cressida*) which seem totally different from all others in the Shakespeare canon. In both *Measure for Measure* and *All's Well That Ends Well* we have a rather unemotional tone and an insistence on a highly legalistic approach to the matter of marriage. At the same time, a great deal of immorality and bawdy material is included, in particular, the "bed-trick." The "bed-trick" occurs when one of the principal characters wishes to go to bed with a woman to whom he is not married for the purposes of gratifying his physical desires. The "trick" consists of substituting another woman who has some legal claim upon the man concerned for the desired lady. Thus, the virtue of the intended victim is preserved, and the legal claim of the other woman is satisfied.

At the same time, each of these plays seems to be imbued with disillusionment about human virtue, and love seems degraded into lust. However, the plays end well as a result of the legalistically planned trick, and those characters who had formerly hated each other are reconciled, and their future happiness is hinted at. Nevertheless, the impression that remains is one of sadness and disillusion, rather than happy reconciliation after many

THE WINTER'S TALE

THE PLAY: The structure of this play has often been criticized because of the gap of sixteen years between Acts III and IV. Other objections have been raised because of the strange way it includes both tragedy and a happy ending. In general, this play ought to be classified among Shakespeare's dramatic romances rather than with the comedies. The factor which permits the latter classification is the happy ending.

It would, however, seem that most objections to *The Winter's Tale* arise from a misunderstanding of the nature of the play. In effect, Shakespeare gives us the complete cycle of a tragic action, as E.M.W. Tillyard points out in *Shakespeare's Last Plays.* We have the beginning of the action in prosperity, the fall into sadness, the attainment of self-knowledge, and, finally, the reconciliation of the hero, in particular, with his environment. In this play, Shakespeare includes the first two parts of tragic action in Acts I-III, and spends the rest of the play working towards the reconciliation. Therefore, the opening portion is condensed.

Again, by the time we come to the last plays of Shakespeare (this play is generally dated 1610-11), the dramatist is moving away from drama in the literal sense. He is now giving us dramas which stand for the cycle of life itself: of birth, of fruitful marriage, and of death. For instance, Perdita is the guiding spirit of fertility and fullness in nature, as the queen, her mother Hermione is the guiding spirit of fruitful marriage and love.

SOURCE AND TEXT: The play is based on Robert Greene's *Pandosto, or the Triumph of Time* (1588). There are definite variations on the source: Shakespeare invented the character of the rogue Autolycus, probably out of his own knowledge of country fairs, and the incident of the statue is not in Greene. The exact source of the statue theme is still a matter of dispute, but Shakespeare, without doubt, drew some of his names from the *Arcadia,* a pastoral novel by Sir Philip Sidney, the perfect gentleman of Elizabeth's court.

The play initially appeared in the First Folio of 1623, and the text is considered good. Obviously, it is a late play because of the indications to be noted in the flexibility of the blank verse with its numerous run-on lines and unaccented final syllables. In its tone, also, the play is close to *The Tempest* and *Cymbeline,* which are generally assigned to the same period of Shakespeare's development.

THE PLOT: Polixenes, King of Bohemia, is visiting his friend, Leontes, King of Sicilia, and his wife, Hermione. After staying nine months, Polixenes gets ready to depart for his own country, but Leontes wishes to keep him longer and he enlists the help of Hermione to induce him to stay. The queen does as she is told in a merry way.

Suddenly, Leontes becomes insanely jealous and suspects that Polixenes and Hermione have been carrying on a love affair. He asks his trusted councilor, Camillo, to poison the visitor; instead, Camillo warns Polixenes, who returns to Bohemia taking Camillo with him.

We then meet Hermoine playing happily with her little son, Mamillius, and discover that she is carrying another child. Leontes rushes in and accuses Hermione of being with child by his former friend, Polixenes. He separates Mamillius from Hermione and throws her into prison to await her trial. In the meantime, he sends messengers to the Oracle at Delphi to find out the truth.

Hermione gives birth to a girl while she is in prison, and Paulina, a lady of the court, takes the child to Leontes in the hope that the infant will soften his heart. The plan fails, and Leontes orders Antigonus, Paulina's husband, to take the child away and expose it on a hostile shore.

When the trial takes place, Hermione argues her case with nobility and wisdom, but Leontes is adamant. He will not even accept the Oracle's statement that Hermione is innocent. Then word is brought that Mamillius, who has been ailing, is dead. Hermione faints. Immediately, Leontes repents, but then word is brought to him that Hermione is also dead.

In the meantime, Antigonus, following orders, exposes the other child, but he follows a dream in which Hermione appeared to him and leaves her on the coast of Bohemia, and, for the same reason, he names her Perdita. As he leaves the child, a great storm arises and his ship is sunk with all hands; he is devoured by a bear. The child, however, is picked up by a rustic and his father, the Shepherd, who decide to take care of her.

Time then appears as a chorus and announces that sixteen years have passed. The next act opens during a sheepshearing feast. We meet Perdita and her lover Florizel, disguised as the shepherd Doricles. Actually, Florizel is the son of Polixenes. The feast continues with laughter and dancing as well as the pickpocketing and general sharp practices of Autolycus, the peddler. Then Polixenes and Camillo, who have been curious to know what Florizel does when away from the court, appear in disguise and question Perdita closely. When Perdita and Florizel are about to become engaged, Polixenes intervenes; he threatens the girl with physical harm and his son with disinheritance. Sadly, the two decide to fly, and Camillo suggests that they go with him to Sicilia. This they do and they are joyfully received by Leontes and his court. In the meantime, the Shepherd and his son, accompanied by Autolycus, have told Polixenes the story of Perdita's past. Polixenes then arrives in Sicilia and a grand recognition scene takes place. Perdita is revealed to her grieving father as his lost child. Happiness abounds except for the absence of Hermione. Leontes is still so repentant that he has not remarried, and has promised not to do so until Paulina, who has been acting as his conscience, gives him permission.

After the joyful reunion with Perdita, Paulina mentions that she has received a finished statue of Hermione that she had commissioned and she invites Leontes and his court to her house to view it. Everyone is amazed at the brilliance of the likeness, especially since the statue seems to represent Hermione at the age she would have been had she lived. Then Paulina calls for music, and the statue comes to life revealing itself as Hermione, who has waited for years to return to her husband. Now there is happiness for all, except for the widowed Paulina. But she, too, as a reward is to be married to the faithful Camillo.

DETAILED SUMMARY OF "THE WINTER'S TALE"

ACT I: SCENE 1

This scene takes place in the antechamber of the palace of Leontes, King of Sicilia, at a remote time in Greek history. (Elizabethans would not have required historical accuracy.) Camillo, a lord of Sicilia, and Archidamus, a lord of Bohemia, are discussing the current visit of Polixenes, King of Bohemia, to Leontes. The friendship of the two kings is praised, and an account of its length and growth is given. Archidamus also praises young Mamillius, Prince of Sicilia.

COMMENT AND SUMMARY: This scene is important as an example of dramatic exposition. Shakespeare swiftly introduces the initial situation, the visit, and the friendship of the two kings, together with praise of the young prince.

ACT I: SCENE 2

This scene takes place in a room of state within Leontes' palace, with an assembled company of Leontes, Hermione, his wife, Mamillius, Polixenes, Camillo, and various attendants. Polixenes opens the proceedings by noting that his visit to Sicilia has now lasted nine months and it is time for him to return to Bohemia. Leontes tries to dissuade him from leaving, and enlists the aid of Hermione to persuade him to remain. Hermione complies, and Polixenes tells of the past friendship between them and remarks that they anticipated life as if it were "to be boy eternal."

COMMENT: This line is important because it shows that, in some respects, this passionate friendship between the kings seems to be based on the rather insecure foundation of childhood dreams. It does not seem to have developed into an adult relationship.

Hermione then proceeds merrily to persuade Polixenes to remain and by exchanging jests with both him and her husband. Suddenly, we see that Leontes does not like what is going on. His attitude starts to resemble that of Othello and we realize, to our surprise, that Leontes is jealous of Polixenes. Indeed, in his words to Mamillius he even questions the honest behavior of Hermione.

COMMENT: The sudden appearance of jealousy in Leontes has been considered a flaw in this play, but Shakespeare has indicated its speedy growth through the King's comments in this scene. The playwright seems, however, to have concentrated on the reconciliation aspect of the tragic cycle of action which begins in prosperity, falls to sorrow, and rises again to reconciliation. As a result, he has compressed motive and manifestation into a single scene. Nevertheless, this precipitate onset of jealousy would have been more easily understood by the Elizabethans than by us, because they would probably have seen it as the sudden onslaught of an aspect of the melancholy humour.

Leontes' jealousy reaches its height in his speech to Mamillius after the departure of Polixenes and Hermione. Then he turns to Camillo, and, after voicing his suspicions as if they had been proved, he demands that his councilor poison Polixenes. Camillo, who is a trifle slow in understanding the changed attitude of Leontes, is appalled, so much so, that he tells Polixenes of the plot against him and the reason for it. The King of Bohemia is shocked, but, at the same time, says that he can understand the violence of Leontes' passion since Hermione is such a rare creature, and since Leontes believes himself betrayed by a friend. With admirable caution, Polixenes decides to leave, and since his ships are ready, his departure is instantaneous.

SUMMARY: This scene constitutes the inciting action of the play—the action from which all future events follow:

1. It displays the friendship between Leontes and Polixenes, but at the same time it hints at a certain immaturity in their relationship.

2. It shows the inception of the jealousy of Leontes. This jealousy is not fully motivated, but a careful study of the scene shows highly compressed indications of its growth.

3. It introduces Hermione as a lady of charm, nobility, and obedience, with a fine, sportive wit.

4. It includes a brief account of Mamillius, who is generally considered to be Shakespeare's best portrait of childhood.

5. It shows us the honesty of Camillo, who, like Kent in *King Lear*, is not afraid to disobey his royal master if he is acting foolishly.

ACT II: SCENE 1

This scene takes place a short time later in another room in Leontes' palace. Hermione, her ladies, and Mamillius are there. At first, Hermione asks one of her ladies to take Mamillius and play with him because his energy has tired her out. The boy then engages in a merry, rather precocious, wit-combat with the ladies, who gladly indulge him. From the conversation of the ladies, we discover that Hermione is about to give birth to another child. Hermione then takes Mamillius back and he starts to tell her a story, "a sad tale's best for winter."

Suddenly, Leontes bursts into this scene of domestic tranquillity to accuse

Hermione of dishonest behavior, going so far as to accuse her of being with child by Polixenes. Hermione does not crumple under the onslaught of words; she answers with consideration, spirit, and politeness. But this mild opposition only enrages her husband more; he orders her to prison. At this point, Hermione resigns herself to the possibility that some evil planet has caused this change in Leontes.

> **COMMENT:** Even today, some persons believe in planetary influences which can bring good or ill to the earth, and can control human behavior.

The Queen is taken away; one lord beseeches Leontes to call her back, but Antigonus, another lord, remains half-convinced of her guilt. Leontes then decides to send to the Oracle at Delphi for confirmation of Hermione's perfidy.

> **COMMENT:** The Oracle at the Temple of Apollo at Delphi was one of the most famous and most trusted in ancient Greece. When statements were given to petitioners, they were usually in the form of ambiguous riddles so that the Oracle's predictions were usually correct as they depended upon interpretations of the riddles.

SUMMARY: This scene carries Leontes' jealousy to a high point and it is also expository.

1. We see Hermione's relationship to her little son.

2. Mamillius's wit and precocity are shown so the child wins the sympathy of the audience. This is the last time we see him in the play.

3. We are told of Hermione's pregnancy, a fact which makes Leontes' suspicion even more distressing. It also gains sympathy for her. Similarly, her rejoinders to her husband show her strength of character, while her resignation when he sends her to prison indicates that she realizes when opposition is impossible. She usually understands Leontes, but this time she is mystified by the change in him.

4. Leontes arranges to send messengers to the Oracle at Delphi.

ACT II: SCENE 2

This scene takes place a short time later within the prison in which Hermione is confined. Paulina, a lady of the court and the wife of Antigonus, enters and inquires after Hermione. Emilia, a lady attendant to the Queen, tells Paulina that she has just given birth prematurely to a daughter. Paulina offers to plead Hermione's cause and asks if she may take the baby to aid her in so doing. Perhaps the sight of the child may melt Leontes' heart. Emilia is doubtful.

COMMENT AND SUMMARY: This brief scene introduces us to the female infant of Hermione, and also to Paulina. Both these characters become important as the play progresses. It also sets up the situation for

Paulina to plead for Hermione and explains in some measure the influence that Paulina has over Leontes later.

ACT II: SCENE 3

This scene takes place in a room in Leontes' palace with Antigonus and assorted lords and servants present. Leontes mutters that he cannot sleep, that Polixenes is beyond his grasp, and that Hermione, the adulteress, offends him by her very existence. He then turns to a servant and inquires after Mamillius. We now discover that the boy is in a decline because of his mother's dishonor. At this moment, Paulina enters carrying the newborn child to plead for Hermione. Leontes is angered with Antigonus for allowing his wife to appear in such wise, but obviously Antigonus has little control over the woman who believes that right is on her side.

> **COMMENT:** In her behavior, Paulina approximates that of Camillo who disobeys his master in a good cause. Like him, she will be shown throughout the play as a person with common sense.

Paulina shows Leontes the child and tells him that it is obviously his own because of its likeness to him. Leontes is only angered further by these pleas and orders Paulina to leave. She obeys, but she leaves the child behind in the hope that it will soften Leontes' heart. However, the opposite attitude results, and Leontes orders Antigonus, on pain of death for both him and his wife, to take the child to a distant land and expose it to the elements. The frightened Antigonus agrees to do Leontes' bidding, although he regrets having to do so.

> **COMMENT:** This exposing of a child to nature, rather than killing it, was a *well-known practice* which is found also in the legend of Oedipus.

Leontes then calls for a session of the court to try Hermione since the messengers sent to the Oracle are due to return. It is twenty-three days since their departure; therefore, the action of the play has so far covered approximately twenty-five days.

> **COMMENT:** It is important to note the passage of time in this play, partly because the action covers such a long period, but, even more important, because Time is, in effect, the ultimate revealer of truth in this play—a revelation which culminates in the final reconciliation.

SUMMARY: This scene is important because of the following plot developments:

1. We hear about Mamillius' illness which arises as a result of his mother's dishonor.

2. We meet Paulina who will defy her husband in a worthy cause.

3. The fate of Hermione's little daughter is decided. She will be exposed on a hostile shore by Antigonus, Paulina's husband.

4. We are told that the messengers from the Oracle are about to return and that Hermione will soon be tried.

ACT III: SCENE 1

This scene takes place at a Sicilian seaport where Cleomenes and Dion, the two messengers, discuss the Oracle. They hope that the statement they bring with them will be helpful to the Queen and they express their faith in the Oracle. They have obvious sympathy for Hermione and disbelieve Leontes.

ACT III: SCENE 2

This scene takes place within a court of justice. Leontes, with his lords and officers in attendance, declares the session open. Hermione is brought in under guard and the charge is read. Hermione is accused of adultery with Polixenes and of conspiring with Camillo to murder Leontes. The flight of Camillo and Polixenes is taken as an admission of their guilt. Hermione replies nobly and eloquently to the charges, which she denies, and says that her love for Polixenes was no more than the law allowed and that it was dictated by Leontes himself. She does not know why Camillo left the court, but she considers him an honest man.

Leontes then accuses her openly of having a bastard daughter by Polixenes, and Hermione replies with the noble temperateness of language we have come to expect of her to deny this charge. She gains our sympathy by saying that she is not permitted to see Mamillius; and, again, by speaking of the newborn baby whom she believes will die; but, most of all, by her openly stated regret at losing the favor of her lord, Leontes. Life means nothing to her after such occurrences.

The words of the Oracle are then read: "Hermione is chaste; Polixenes blameless; Camillo a true subject; Leontes a jealous tyrant; his innocent babe truly begotten; and the king shall live without an heir, if that which is lost be not found." This statement is plain enough, but Leontes is so blinded by his anger, passion, and jealousy, that he will permit no one, not even the Oracle to contradict him.

At this moment, a servant enters to announce the death of Mamillius. Hermione, still weak from childbirth, swoons, and is carried away by Paulina and the ladies. Almost immediately, Leontes repents and wants to forgive Polixenes and Camillo.

> **COMMENT:** This sudden repentance has, like the sudden onset of Leontes' jealousy, been criticized. According to Elizabethan psychology, a sudden shock could have caused Leontes' humours to return to their natural balance so that the predominance of the humour which had caused his anger and jealousy would be overcome.

Paulina enters to announce the death of Hermione. She upbraids Leontes for his cruelty and wanton suspicion. The King orders that his wife and son be buried together and that an account of the circumstances of their death should appear on their tomb—to his own eternal shame. He promises to visit the chapel of their grave daily to mourn his loss.

SUMMARY: This scene serves the following purposes:

1. It gives Hermione a chance to plead her own case so that she gains sympathy. At her death, she has the love of all.

2. Through the death of Mamillius, it shows the frightful result of unbridled passion.

3. It shows the repentance of Leontes, although it is apparently too late, as he seems to have fallen into grief.

4. It presents the statement of the Oracle which points forward to the remaining action of the play, as well as confirming Hermione's innocence.

5. It gives some indication of the part that Paulina will play during the rest of the action, when she acts as the conscience of the King.

ACT III: SCENE 3

This scene takes place in a desert area of Bohemia near the sea. Antigonus enters with the child and a sailor. The mariner remarks on the threatening weather and Antigonus sends him back to the ship while he, with regret, leaves Hermione's child. As he lays her on the ground, he tells of a dream in which Hermione appeared to him as he was about to leave Sicilia and begged him to expose her child on the shore of its father's country, Bohemia, and to call it Perdita, since it is lost forever. Obviously, Antigonus believes in Hermione's guilt, but he does as the dream asked. As he turns to leave under the lowering sky, a bear pursues him.

> **COMMENT:**   Although Antigonus apparently believes in the guilt of Hermione, his care to follow out the instructions in his dream show his innate kindness. Shakespeare has been laughed at for giving Bohemia a sea coast, but, instead of being an error, it may be merely an Elizabethan expression to signify a remote region.

A rustic clown appears and calls for his father, a shepherd. The rustic then tells of the devouring of Antigonus by the bear, and, also, of the vessel he has just seen wrecked with the loss of all hands. As they walk along, they find the child, Perdita, and note that it is noble by its dress. The Shepherd, recalling that he had been told he "should be rich by fairies," considers the child a changeling and he takes her into his house.

SUMMARY: This scene is important for its influence on the later development of the play.

1. It disposes of Antigonus and all the witnesses. At least, he did try to do the best thing possible for the child, while still obeying Leontes' orders.

2. It places Perdita among shepherds who lead a simple life close to the heart of nature.

ACT IV: SCENE 1

Time enters as a chorus to recount all that has happened during the sixteen years which had intervened. Leontes has retired from the world in grief. Polixenes has a son, Prince Florizel, and Perdita has grown into a girl of grace living among the shepherds.

> **COMMENT:** This lapse of time has been criticized, but it is essential if Shakespeare is to give us the complete cycle of life. The use of a chorus is not new to Shakespeare but, in dressing him as Time, he indicates the importance of the triumph of Time in the reconciliation theme of the entire play.

ACT IV: SCENE 2

This scene takes place in the palace of Polixenes where the King is trying to dissuade Camillo from returning to Sicilia. Camillo wishes to see his native land after his long absence, and, further, Leontes has asked him to return. However, the King of Bohemia is disturbed about the behavior of his son, and Camillo confirms his frequent absences from court. Polixenes has also heard that Florizel seems to be spending his time at the house of a poor shepherd who, as Camillo notes, has an extremely beautiful daughter. Polixenes then suggests that he and Camillo disguise themselves in order to observe what is going on. Camillo agrees.

COMMENT AND SUMMARY: This short scene is primarily expository. It brings us up to date on the repentance of Leontes, and also on the actions of Florizel, pointing forward to the future love interest of the play.

ACT IV: SCENE 3

In this scene, a road near the Shepherd's cottage, we meet Autolycus, the wandering peddler, who is the only rogue in the play. He is merry and musical, and continually speaks of the tricks he has played on gullible folk. He is evil-in-the-making, but most of the tricks he plays are relatively harmless.

COMMENT AND SUMMARY: Autolycus is a merry character who is the nearest approach to real evil in the play. He is a realistically drawn rogue who seems to come right out of the underworld. He prevents the pleasant world of the shepherds from becoming a place of cloying sweetness and he assumes importance in the concluding action of the play.

ACT IV: SCENE 4

This scene takes place at the Shepherd's cottage where Florizel and Perdita are walking together. She is in festive dress, and is so bedecked with flowers that Florizel considers her to be the goddess Flora. Perdita humbly

turns aside such excessive praise, but Florizel gives thanks that he chanced
to meet Perdita when his hunting falcon flew across the Shepherd's land.
Perdita is afraid of meeting Florizel's father, but the young man is con-
fident that his father knows nothing about their affair. Gods, he says, have
changed their shapes for mortals less fair than Perdita. Florizel then declares his love, despite the opposition of his father. At that moment, the
Shepherd appears, accompanied by the Clown, Mopsa and Dorcas, two
country wenches, and Polixenes and Camillo in disguise. The old Shepherd
rebukes his daughter, Perdita, for neglecting her duties as hostess.

> **COMMENT:** This opening rebuke also helps dilute the excessive
> idealism of the world of the shepherds. The pastoral tradition, which
> began in Sicily, was a double one which included both a delight in
> the virtue resulting from the primitive closeness to the earth in an
> idealized, simple life, and also a criticism of the life of the civilized
> world, particularly that of the court. Reality is never far removed
> from the pastoral world. From now on, we must accept much of
> the play's action in a nonliteral way.

Perdita obediently welcomes the guests, Polixenes and Camillo, giving
them sprigs of rosemary (remembrance) and rue (regret), plants suitable
for their ages. They then engage her in a discussion of nature and art.
Perdita expresses her belief in the superiority of nature as it actually is,
and not as man has made use of it or altered it into such things as hybrid
plants. The King, however, comes out in favor of art, the grafting of a
baser, but stronger, plant on to that of a more beautiful, yet weaker one
in order to gain the advantages of both. Perdita disagrees quite vehemently.

> **COMMENT:** This scene contains aspects of the great Renaissance
> debate between natural nature (*natura naturans*) and nature as it is
> used and changed by man (*natura naturata*). In this scene, its ap-
> plication to the relationship between Perdita and Florizel is clear.
> The young girl also takes on some of the attributes of Proserpina,
> the daughter of Cybele, who returns to earth in the spring, and is
> the patroness of fertility.

Polixenes and Camillo are impressed with Perdita, and the King remarks
that she seems too noble to come from the hut of a shepherd.

> **COMMENT:** It was believed that noble birth would always show
> itself, even in the humblest circumstances. For instance, in *As You
> Like It,* Oliver, the cruel brother of Orlando, refuses his younger
> brother any sort of education and civilized training, yet he is obvi-
> ously a gentleman.

Perdita and Florizel, who goes under the name of Doricles, then exchange
words of love, and the shepherds and shepherdesses dance around. Polixenes makes inquiries of the Shepherd to see how much he knows of the
identity of Doricles, but the Shepherd evidently believes him to be a pros-
perous young shepherd. He also hints at a secret concerning Perdita. At
this point, a servant announces the arrival of Autolycus, the peddler, who

sings merrily, sells his goods to the girls, and ballads to those who wish to sing them after they have heard his renditions. The rustics are also engaged in wooing each other, and we find the Clown wooing Mopsa. The ballad singing is followed by a dance of twelve Satyrs (probably jumpers) who have performed before the King.

The disguised Polixenes then begins to talk to Florizel about his not buying gifts from the peddler for Perdita, and the young man speaks of Perdita's joy in spiritual gifts rather than in the things a peddler has to sell. He praises the beauty of his lady even more highly, then takes Perdita's hand and the Shepherd promptly promises his daughter to him. They commence their betrothal, but Polixenes asks whether the young man intends to get his father's consent. Florizel says no. In anger, Polixenes reveals himself and turns on Perdita, threatening her with disfigurement and forbidding Florizel ever to see her again.

> **COMMENT:** Note the way the sudden anger of Polixenes largely parallels that of Leontes. There is also some irony since Polixenes had already praised the grafting of baser stock on to a finer plant.

Perdita, in a manner reminiscent of Hermione, claims that she is not afraid, and, indeed, that she had thought to tell the King that the same sun shines on each of them. Florizel then resolves on flight with Perdita, and, after trying to dissuade him, the sympathetic Camillo offers to help them flee to Sicilia where he is sure they will receive welcome.

Autolycus again appears and speaks merrily of the tricks he has played during the earlier part of the scene. Then Camillo has Florizel change clothes with the peddler as a disguise. The little group then leaves, Autolycus congratulating himself on his exchange. At this point, the Shepherd and Clown enter, the latter telling his father that they have to tell the King the truth about Perdita. The Shepherd agrees and says that they will go to the King and tell him also about the behavior of Florizel. Autolycus, with an eye to mischief, then offers himself in his fine clothes as a courtier and a suitable escort for the rustics who innocently answer all his leading questions. Autolycus states his ultimate dilemma: even if he wished to be honest, Fortune puts dishonesty in his way, and he must obey.

SUMMARY: This scene is the most important in the play for its advancement of the plot, for its changes of tone, and for its intellectual and philosophical content.

1. It introduces us to the world of pastoral where things are not to be taken literally much of the time, but as standing for something else—in this case, the world at large.

2. It introduces two great Renaissance conflicts of thought: nature opposed to art, and the source of true nobility—breeding or upbringing.

3. It shows us Perdita, who, in her behavior is a younger Hermione, as a kind of goddess of fertility and love.

4. It introduces Florizel, son of Polixenes and the lover of Perdita.

5. It includes the wrath of Polixenes at the proposed match of his son with the simple maiden. This situation parallels the earlier jealousy of Leontes.

6. In another parallel situation, Camillo offers to help the couple escape from Polixenes' wrath by going to Sicilia.

7. By having the Shepherd and the Clown decide to go to Polixenes, it hastens the untangling of the complex plot. And, by having them meet with Autolycus, a certain delay in the discovery is assured.

ACT V: SCENE 1

We return to Leontes' palace in Sicilia, where we find the King, Cleomenes, Dion, Paulina, and servants. Cleomenes, who had been one of the messengers to the Oracle, is trying to persuade Leontes to cease his mourning and repentance. Dion goes further by suggesting that Leontes ought to remarry for the good of the state, so that the government of Sicilia will pass to a lawful heir without political disturbance.

> **COMMENT:** This topic was an important one in the days of Queen Elizabeth who had kept the name of her heir secret until her deathbed. History had shown Englishmen that a disputed succession to the throne could breed civil war.

But every argument put forward by the two men is foiled by Paulina who speaks glowingly of Hermione, thereby increasing the grief of Leontes. Finally, Paulina gets him to swear that he will never take another wife without *her* permission.

A servant then appears to announce the arrival of Florizel and a girl who is "The fairest I have yet beheld." On hearing this remark, Paulina laments that Hermione should be so soon forgotten. Cleomenes and others are sent to bring the young couple in. Leontes laments the fact that he has lost his own two children who would have been about the same age. Florizel presents fictitious greetings from Polixenes and all seems well until a lord enters with orders from Polixenes that his son and Perdita be held prisoner. They have been followed: Polixenes is in Sicilia, accompanied by Autolycus, the Shepherd, and the Clown. Florizel immediately concludes that Camillo has betrayed them both, especially when he hears that the councilor is with the royal party. Leontes, on discovering that the couple are not yet married, delivers Florizel a homily on filial duty, but the young man begs him for help. Leontes finds himself surprised into an admission of interest in Perdita for himself, but is immediately admonished by Paulina to think of Hermione. Ironically, Leontes says that he had, in fact, been doing just that while gazing at Perdita.

SUMMARY: This scene is important because it engineers the arrival of the principal characters in Sicilia simultaneously.

1. It shows the repentance of Leontes, and, at this time, we feel sympathy

for the sincerity of such long sorrowing. Paulina, to our surprise, gets the King to agree not to marry without her permission. She is testing Leontes' repentance.

2. Cleomenes and Dion, by arguing that it is Leontes' duty to remarry indicate that the King will even sacrifice his kingdom for his repentance and love for the dead Hermione.

3. Perdita is subconsciously recognized both by the gentleman who announces her arrival, and by Leontes who feels love towards her, but mistakes its stimulation.

4. Polixenes, the Shepherd, the Clown, and Camillo arrive. Shakespeare defers any marriage scene.

ACT V: SCENE 2

This scene takes place outside the palace of Leontes. Autolycus and a gentleman enter; then two more gentlemen arrive. All have just come from inside the palace and can talk of nothing but the astonishing scene in which the identity of Perdita has just been revealed as the result of the evidence found in Perdita's baby clothes and identification which the Shepherd had kept for such a possibility. The entire action of the past sixteen years has been recounted, including the death of Antigonus and the drowning of the crew of the ship which had brought Perdita to Bohemia. Apparently, it was both a memorably merry and sorrowful occasion.

> **COMMENT:** Note that the actual recognition and account of the past takes place offstage. This device has been criticized, but it is really a fine example of dramatic economy. The audience already knows the facts, and also this recognition scene would detract from the final one which follows.

We are then told that Paulina has promised to take Leontes and the company to her house to see a statue of Hermione which has just been completed for her by Julio Romano (he is an anachronism since he was a sculptor of Shakespeare's day).

The Shepherd and the Clown enter, the young man rejoicing that the King has now declared them to be gentlemen. The Clown makes comments at the expense of courtly morality, but the Shepherd declares that he will stick to the familiar honest usages of the country. In this attitude, he is shown as typifying the honesty of ideal shepherds uncorrupted by civilization.

SUMMARY: This scene contains an account of the recognition of Perdita, and of the events of the past sixteen years. It includes Paulina's promise to take the company to show the company a lifelike statue of Hermione. The Shepherd and his son are rewarded. Everything is now ready for the final recognition scene.

ACT V: SCENE 3

This scene takes place in a chapel in the house of Paulina. Leontes, Polixenes, Florizel, Perdita, Camillo, Paulina, and a crowd of lords and attendants have assembled. Leontes is impatient to see the statue and Paulina draws back the curtains to disclose Hermione standing as if she were a sculptured figure. The repentant King gazes on her with sorrow and joy, but then notes with wonderment that Hermione looks more wrinkled in this statue than when he saw her last. To this objection, Paulina answers that the artist has carved Hermione as she would have been had she lived. Perdita wishes to touch the statue, and Leontes wishes to kiss it. Paulina refuses permission, but then she says that she can make it move from its pedestal, *but not through wicked powers*. She then calls for music, and Hermione comes down to embrace her husband. Paulina then tells the Queen that Perdita is her daughter and the entire company rejoices.

> **COMMENT:** The device of the statue is an old one, and Shakespeare uses it here in addition to his main source. It had been used before in Elizabethan drama. Certainly, it is a fine piece of stage suspense which culminates in recognition.

Paulina then comments on her own widowhood, and Leontes offers her Camillo as a husband. The King admires both of them for their loyalty to Hermione and, therefore, he foresees a fine match. So the play ends happily with complete reconciliation and three happy couples.

COMMENT AND SUMMARY: Note that Paulina says " 'Tis time," when she bids the supposed statue of Hermione awaken, and at the end of the play Leontes speaks of what has happened in the sixteen-year passage of time. In a sense, Time is predominant in this play. Through the passage of time, truth is revealed, and rewards are given to those who, like Leontes, have erred, but who have finally reached self-knowledge and reconciliation. This scene is the highest point of action in the play; all the knots are untied; the words of the Oracle have been fulfilled, and sadness is banished.

CHARACTER ANALYSES:
"THE WINTER'S TALE"

LEONTES: As King of Sicily, he really initiates the action of the play. His temper is short, and both his jealousy and his repentance are sudden. Leontes' jealous temper, which the Elizabethans would have seen as being caused by the imbalance of humours or bodily fluids, is immediately removed by the shock of the death of Mamillius and replaced by grief at the "death" of Hermione. But, since his repentance has been so rapid, it must also be prolonged. Consequently, he must undergo a long period of probation before the truth is revealed to him. By the end of the play, his sorrow has taught him self-knowledge.

POLIXENES: He is the King of Bohemia, and a great friend of Leontes, whom, in some ways, he resembles. His anger with Florizel over his match with Perdita is comparable to the jealousy of Leontes. This passion, however, does not have quite the same serious consequences, and when he learns the truth about Perdita, reconciliation with his son is inevitable.

HERMIONE: She is a gentle, yet firm, womanly character. Throughout the play she behaves with royal dignity. When she must defend herself against the accusations of Leontes, she never becomes angry, but, instead, marshals her points with skill and argues well. She is a realistically drawn character, and possesses a sportive wit and a good sense of humor at the beginning of the play when she is persuading Polixenes to remain. In many ways, she is the most memorable character of the play.

PERDITA: She is, in every way, a daughter worthy of Hermione. Her honesty and virtue are unassailable, and her beauty is remarkable. So also is her courage, because she argues with Polixenes in as precise a manner as her mother had displayed with Leontes. She is courageous and self-possessed, and is not terrified by Polixenes' threats. Due to her high birth, she possesses natural nobility, which has been increased as the result of living a pastoral life close to nature. In some ways, she exists on a nonliteral level, having inner qualities like the goddess of fertility and increase.

FLORIZEL: He is not drawn very fully as a character, but he is a pleasant enough young lover with a youthful belief that true love will surmount all obstacles. His optimism is justified when, finally, he does marry his Perdita.

MAMILLIUS: As Leontes' only son who dies early in the play, he is not a prominent character. Nevertheless, he remains in memory as Shakespeare's best picture of childhood. He is precocious, but not too much so, and his death increases our sympathy for Hermione, and arouses our anger towards Leontes.

CAMILLO: He, like King Lear's servant, Kent, is loyal to Leontes, but he refuses to follow his master when he acts foolishly. He remains constantly a norm of virtue and good sense in the play, because he also helps Florizel and Perdita when Polixenes, in his turn, is acting foolishly. His reward of marriage to Paulina seems well merited.

PAULINA: She is the companion character representing good sense and loyalty in the play. Above all things, she is loyal to her mistress, and she acts as the conscience of Leontes during the sixteen years that Hermione remains hidden. She is strong-minded and gifted with a good sense of rhetoric. Her marriage to the lightly drawn Antigonus seems pleasant enough, but her second marriage to Camillo seems destined for true happiness.

AUTOLYCUS: This peddler seems a character who has come straight out of personal observation of the English countryside and the seventeenth-century underworld. He is a frequenter of feasts and fairs where he sells his wares, picks pockets, and steals keys on the side. No maiden is safe with him—to hear him tell us of his exploits. He is a rogue, but a realistic and a merry one. His gaiety is infectious, and, at the end of the play, he has some part in the final recognition. He seems congenitally dishonest, and' claims that no matter how hard he tries to be virtuous, Fortune puts such fine possibilities for dishonesty in his way that he cannot refuse them. He is the nearest approach to evil in the play.

ESSAY QUESTIONS FOR REVIEW: "THE WINTER'S TALE"

1. What important Renaissance arguments and themes are to be found in this play?

The major themes discussed in this highly intellectual and symbolic play include friendship, evil, virtue, love, nature versus art, nobility, and education.

The first of these themes is embodied in the chapters of Leontes and Polixenes, but their friendship is an imperfect one because it appears to be based on an insecure foundation—that of eternal boyhood. As a result, this friendship cannot stand, and it is temporarily broken because of the unfounded suspicion and jealousy of Leontes, who, in this situation, also stands for evil. Leontes' suspicion and anger are paralleled later by Polixenes when he threatens to disown his son, Florizel, and to harm Perdita. Both of these men are temporarily blinded by their rage and passion and act in an unreasonable manner. Luckily, except for the death of Mamillius, the results of their evil is not completely irreversible. Evil is also embodied in the carnival character of Autolycus. But he is a merry man, and, although he talks a great deal about his prowess with women, we do not see evidence of it. Instead, we hear of the tricks he has played on the unsophisticated rustics. He is congenitally dishonest, but his crimes are generally minor ones of fraud and theft.

Virtue and love are represented by Hermione and her daughter, Perdita, who possess great dignity and courage in the face of adversity. Hermione is the innocent victim of Leontes, as Perdita is the victim of the rage of Polixenes. Perdita also represents nature in the debate between nature and art which she, herself, discusses with Polixenes. She is a goddesslike figure of love and fertility, and she stands for the supremacy of unaltered nature, while Polixenes, older and more civilized, favors nature when used and changed by man for his own purposes. Polixenes particularly supports the practice of grafting stronger, and baser, stock on to a weaker, but nobler, strain. The irony of this attitude is obvious because Polixenes later refuses to allow such intermingling to occur in his own family. Florizel is refused permission to marry his Perdita who, since she appears to be a shepherdess, is considered to be too low in rank for a prince.

One other allied aspect is also included in this play, the problem of nature opposed to nurture. Perdita possesses true virtue, as she is born of noble line, and this nobility is reinforced by her honest life away from the sophisticated, courtly world. As a result, she is better educated in virtue, the true nobility, than anyone at the court of Bohemia.

2. This play has been criticized for its structure. Why should this be so, and what was Shakespeare apparently trying to do?

The major flaw which the critics have detected in this play is the fact that it covers such a long period of time. Between Acts III and IV, one is asked to believe that sixteen years have passed. The play, therefore, seems to fall into two separate parts—the first concerned with the matter of Leontes and Hermione; and the second with the love affair of Perdita and Florizel, together with the final reconciliation.

It would appear that in this play Shakespeare is giving us the complete tragice cycle, showing us Leontes' fall from high estate through an error of judgment on his own part. But instead of leaving him in a state of self-knowledge and sorrow Shakespeare goes on to show us the final reconciliation which invariably ends a complete tragic action. Such a conclusion is usually a spiritual one, but here Shakespeare has made it a physical and terrestrial one, but, like its philosophical, and even mystical, counterpart it implies a moral recognition and a period of repentance.

3. What is the importance of Time in this play?

Time appears only as a Chorus at the beginning of Act IV, yet, in many ways, his influence pervades the play. The source of the play bears the subtitle "The Triumph of Time" and, indeed, the play itself may be read in this manner. "Truth is the daughter of Time," it is said, and it is only as a result of the passage of time that the truth is finally brought to light. With the revelation of the truth of human behavior, the final reconciliation can take place and Leontes' repentance can receive an earthly reward and forgiveness because Hermione is discovered to be alive.

With this play, Shakespeare goes beyond the literal interpretation of incidents played before us on the stage. He is moving towards symbolic drama in which events carry a deeper meaning than is first apparent. This new approach reaches its height in Shakespeare's last major play, *The Tempest*.

CRITICAL COMMENTARY

GENERAL: The criticism of Shakespeare's comedies does not bulk as large as that devoted to the tragedies, and it is difficult to sort out various schools of thought and lines of development. The comedies seem to have been popular in their own day, and, in 1598, Francis Meres, a contemporary of Shakespeare, praised him as "the most excellent" English dramatist in both tragedy and comedy. Despite this praise, one may say that, generally, the early comedies, the "problem plays," and the dramatic romances (with the exception of *The Tempest*) were considered inferior Shakespeare in the seventeenth an deighteenth centuries. Some of them were not produced again before the end of this period, but about the only one discussed in this book which achieved popularity was *The Merry Wives of Windsor,* probably because of the character of Falstaff.

REPUTATION OF SHAKESPEARE'S COMEDIES: The early comedies disappeared from critical consideration, so it is hard to find interest in them as a group until the end of the nineteenth century when they were revived on stage. Edward Dowden saw them as embracing two periods of Shakespeare's development: "In the Workshop" and "In the World"; but, in general, they were considered apprentice work aimed at making the audience in the cheapest part of the theatre, the groundlings, laugh. A further difficulty arises from the nature of comedy itself. One rarely knows how seriously one should take a comic drama because the author may have intended mockery—even of the critic who tries to disentangle the philosophy from the laughter.

TWENTIETH-CENTURY CRITICISM: As a result, it has been left largely to the twentieth century to examine the comedies as a group of plays. Some comments and studies did appear in the nineteenth century, but they were often based largely on a romantic approach rather than on solid critical theory. Even today, it is difficult to find any ground-breaking study comparable to Bradley's *Shakespearean Tragedy* (1904) which has influenced criticism of the comedies to a marked degree. Studies of single plays seem to follow a pattern: source study, background study, textual criticism, and general critical inquiry on individual points, such as Shakespeare's debt to Italian *commedia dell'arte* (popular, improvised comedy). Specific themes have also been studied, most notably that of love. C.H. Herford, in *Shakespeare's Treatment of Love and Marriage* (London, 1921) commented on the playwright's completely "normal" approach to love-making which usually ends in marriage. Attempts have also been made to include the comedies in the tradition of courtly entertainment, but with less success.

One of the most important early critiques of "Shakespeare as a comic dramatist" appeared in a chapter on the subject by Edward Dowden in C.M. Gayley's *Representative English Comedies* (New York, 1903). Dowden concluded that Shakespeare ought not to be taken as a satiric comic writer, but, instead, should be praised for his sane outlook on life, his control of the passions, and his moral wisdom. This attitude was countered by O. J. Campbell in *Shakespeare's Satire* (London, 1943).

Ashley Thorndike in *English Comedy* (New York, 1929) followed Dowden and thought the plays should be taken as mere gaiety without any underlying satirical meaning. The same approach is to be found in J. Dover Wilson, *Shakespeare's Happy Comedies* (London, 1962), which takes Shakespeare's comedy to be one concerning the emotions rather than reformation.

G. Wilson Knight in *The Shakespearian Tempest* (London, 1932) and *The Crown of Life* (London, 1943) has made some very perceptive and intuitive comments on the comedies, particularly on *The Winter's Tale*, in the latter volume. As a reaction to romantic criticism of all kinds, E.E. Stoll in *Art and Artifice in Shakespeare* (Cambridge, England, 1933) insisted on the overriding importance of the dramatic situation. H.B. Charlton in *Shakespearian Comedy* (London, 1938) followed the same moral approach as in Bradley's study of tragedy and spoke of the way Shakespeare "sought to elucidate the moral art of securing happiness." Alfred Harbage in *As They Liked It* (New York, 1947) also discussed Shakespeare and morality, concluding that the comedies aimed at "the enjoyment of life in the simplest and most available ways." Comments on individual plays may be found in T.M. Parrott's *Shakespearean Comedy* (New York, 1949).

THE PHILOSOPHY OF SHAKESPEAREAN COMEDY: At the same time, attempts have been made to discover a coherent Shakespearean philosophy of comedy. In 1948, Northrop Frye, in an essay, "The Argument of Comedy," drew attention to Shakespeare's debt to folk plays, rituals, and classical and Renaissance drama in general. Two years later, Nevill Coghill in his essay, "The basis of Shakespearian Comedy," discussed medieval affinities with Shakespeare's drama, and noted that, like Dante's *Divina Commedia*, the plays usually begin in sorrow and end in joy, reached by a poetic course. S.C. Sen Gupta in *Shakespearian Comedy* (Calcutta, 1950) is, on the whole, the most successful critic in establishing a basic philosophy for Shakespeare's comedy; he sees it as a pattern of contrasts rather than conflicts. John Palmer in *Comic Characters of Shakespeare* (London, 1946) carried the study of specific characters to the furthest point yet, while Northrop Frye in his "Characterization in Shakespearean Comedy" (1953) discusses the use of stock characters. In 1958, E.M.W. Tillyard, in an English Association address, *The Nature of Comedy and Shakespeare* (London), discussed the various approaches Shakespeare used in his plays, as also did John Russell Brown in *Shakespeare and His Comedies* (London, 1957). The approach which treats the plays as individual entities finds a sound champion in D.A. Traversi, *An Approach to Shakespeare* (New York, 1956), while M.C. Bradbrook in *The Growth and Structure of Elizabethan Comedy* (London, 1961) relates Shakespere to the other comic writers of his age.

BACKGROUND AND SOURCE STUDIES: The backgrounds of the comedies have also been studied, and Shakespeare's debt to the romance tradition discussed by E.C. Pettet in *Shakespeare and the Romance Tradition* (London, 1949). A more general discussion is presented by Karl J. Holzknecht in *The Backgrounds of Shakespeare's Plays* (New York,

1950). The possible sources for the plays are currently being re-evaluated by Geoffrey Bullough in *Narrative and Dramatic Sources of Shakespeare* (London, 1957). Topical references are sought in a variety of plays, notably in *Love's Labour's Lost* and *The Merry Wives of Windsor*.

THE PROBLEM COMEDIES: There has always been more work on the so-called "problem comedies" than on the earlier plays, and W.W. Lawrence's *Shakespeare's Problem Comedies* (New York, 1931) pointed out the folklore background in *All's Well That Ends Well* as well as examining the problems of the bed-trick. His successor in dealing with these plays is E.M.W. Tillyard in *Shakespeare's Problem Plays* (London, 1950).

THE LAST PLAYS: Tillyard is also the author of a distinguished work, *Shakespeare's Last Plays* (London, 1951), in which he treats the final works as having meaning on more than one level and as a statement of the entire tragic cycle of action. In a full-length study of *The Winter's Tale* (New York, 1947), S.L. Bethell studies the play against a background of Christian tradition and the reconciliation of opposites. More recently, D.A. Traversi in *Shakespeare: The Last Phase* (New York, 1955) has brought his acute sensibility and critical intelligence to a study of the plays as symbolic drama.

CONCLUSION: Criticism of the comedies has not completely solidified, and there is still material which is obscure and not easily available. In summary, the generally accepted over-all theories of Shakespearean comedy agree on its humanity, its happy atmosphere, and its absence of openly reforming zeal. Shakespeare apparently created a unique synthesis of the various elements of comedy and fused them into what may well be called "human" comedy.

BIBLIOGRAPHY

I. GENERAL STUDIES.

Bradbrook, M.C. *The Growth and Structure of Elizabethan Comedy*. London: Chatto and Windus, 1961.

Bradley, A.C. *Shakespearean Tragedy*. London: Macmillan, 1904.

Brown, John Russell. "The Interpretation of Shakespeare's Comedies: 1900-1953," *Shakespeare Survey* 8 (1955), 1-13.

————. *Shakespeare and His Comedies*. London: Methuen, 1957.

Bullough, Geoffrey. *Narrative and Dramatic Sources of Shakespeare*. London: Routledge and Paul, 1957-, 3 vols.

Charlton, H.B. *Shakespearian Comedy*. New York: Macmillan, 1938.

Coghill, Nevill. "The Basis of Shakespearian Comedy," *Essays and Studies*, III (1950), 1-28.

Dowden, Edward. "Shakespeare as a Comic Dramatist" in C.M. Gayley, *Representative English Comedies*. New York: Macmillan, 1903, I, 637-661.

Frye, Northrop. "The Argument of Comedy," *English Institute Essays*, 1948, 58-73.

————. "Characterization in Shakespearian Comedy," *Shakespeare Quarterly*, IV (1953), 271-277.

Gordon, George S. *Shakespearian Comedy and Other Studies*. London: Oxford University Press, 1944.

Harbage, Alfred. *As They Liked It*. New York: Macmillan, 1947.

Herford, C.H. *Shakespeare's Treatment of Love and Marriage and Other Essays*. London: T.F. Unwin, 1921.

Holzknecht, Karl J. *The Backgrounds of Shakespeare's Plays*. New York: American Book Co., 1950.

Knight, G. Wilson. *The Shakespearian Tempest*. London: Humphrey Milford, Oxford University Press, 1932.

Parrott, Thomas Marc. *Shakespearean Comedy*. New York: Oxford University Press, 1949.

Pettet, E.C. *Shakespeare and the Romance Tradition*. London: Staples, 1949.

Sen Gupta, S.C. *Shakespearian Comedy*. Calcutta: Geoffrey Cumberlege, Oxford University Press, 1950.

Stoll, E.E. *Art and Artifice in Shakespeare*. Cambridge (England): University Press, 1933.

Thorndike, Ashley. *English Comedy*. New York: Macmillan, 1929.

Tillyard, E.M.W. *The Nature of Comedy and Shakespeare*. London: Oxford University Press, 1958. [English Association Presidential Address, 1958.]

Traversi, Derek A. *An Approach to Shakespeare*, 2nd ed. Garden City, New York: Doubleday Anchor, 1956.

————. *William Shakespeare: The Early Comedies*. London: Longmans Green for the British Council, 1960.

Wilson, J. Dover. *Shakespeare's Happy Comedies*. London: Faber, 1962.

II. "ALL'S WELL THAT ENDS WELL."

Adams, John F. "*All's Well That Ends Well*: The Paradox of Procreation," *Shakespeare Quarterly*, XII (1961), 261-270.

Arthos, John. "The Comedy of Generation," *Essays in Criticism*, V (1955), 97-117.

Carter, Albert H. "In Defense of Bertram," *Shakespeare Quarterly*, VII (1956), 21-31.

Lawrence, W.W. *Shakespeare's Problem Comedies*. New York: Macmillan, 1931.

Leech, Clifford. "The Theme of Ambition in *All's Well That Ends Well*," *ELH*, XXI (1954), 17-29.

Nagarajan S. "The Structure of *All's Well That Ends Well*," *Essays in Criticism*, X (1960), 24-31.

Ranald, Margaret L. "The Betrothals of *All's Well That Ends Well*," *Huntington Library Quarterly*, XXVI (1963), 179-192.

Tillyard, E.M.W. *Shakespeare's Problem Plays*. London: Chatto and Windus, 1950.

Turner, Robert Y. "Dramatic Convention in *All's Well That Ends Well*," *PMLA*, LXXV (1960), 497-502.

Ure, Peter. *William Shakespeare: The Problem Plays*. London: Longmans Green for the British Council, 1961.

Wilson, Harold. "Dramatic Emphasis in *All's Well That Ends Well*," *Huntington Library Quarterly*, XIII (1950), 222-240.

III. "THE COMEDY OF ERRORS."

Brooks, Charles. "Shakespeare's Romantic Shrews," *Shakespeare Quarterly*, XI (1960), 351-356. [Adriana and Katharina.]

Brooks, Harold. "Themes and Structure in *The Comedy of Errors*" in *Early Shakespeare*. New York: St. Martin's Press, 1961. [Stratford-upon-Avon Studies, No. 3.]

Fergusson, Francis. "*Comedy of Errors* and *Much Ado About Nothing*," *Sewanee Review*, LXII (1954), 24-37.

Gaw, Allison. "The Evolution of *The Comedy of Errors*," *PMLA*, XLI (1926), 620-666.

IV. "LOVE'S LABOUR'S LOST."

Campbell, O.J. "*Love's Labour's Lost* Restudied," *Studies in Shakespeare, Milton, and Donne*. Ann Arbor [Mich.]: University of Michigan Press, 1925, 3-45.

Granville-Barker, Harley. *Prefaces to Shakespeare*. 2nd series. Princeton, N.J.: University Press, 1947.

Oakeshott, Walter. *The Queen and the Poet*. London: Faber, 1960.

Palmer, John. *Comic Characters of Shakespeare*. London: Macmillan, 1946.

Stevenson, D.L. *The Love-Game Comedy*. New York: Columbia University Press, 1946.

Yates, Frances A. *A Study of Love's Labour's Lost*. Cambridge (England): University Press, 1936.

V. "THE MERRY WIVES OF WINDSOR."

Bracy, William. *The Merry Wives of Windsor: The History and Transmission of Shakespeare's Text*. Columbia, Missouri: University of Missouri Studies, XXV, No. 1, 1952.

Campbell, O.J. "The Italianate Background of *The Merry Wives of Windsor*," *Essays and Studies in English and Comparative Literature*. University of Michigan Publications in Language and Literature, VIII (1932), 81-117.

Green, William. *Shakespeare's Merry Wives of Windsor*. Princeton, N.J.: University Press, 1961.

Hotson, J. Leslie. *Shakespeare Versus Shallow*. Boston: Little, Brown, 1931.

VI. "THE TAMING OF THE SHREW."

Bradbrook, M.C. "Dramatic Role as Social Image: A Study of *The Taming of the Shrew*," *Shakespeare Jahrbuch*, XCIV (1958), 132-150.

Duthie, G.I. "*The Taming of A Shrew* and *The Taming of The Shrew*," *Review of English Studies*, XIX (1948), 337-356.

Kuhl, E.P. "The Authorship of *The Taming of the Shrew*," *PMLA*, XL (1927), 551-618.

Seronsy, C.C. "*Supposes* as the Unifying Theme in *The Shrew*," *Shakespeare Quarterly*, XIV (1963), 15-30.

Wentersdorf, K. "The Authenticity of *The Taming of the Shrew*," *Shakespeare Quarterly*, V (1954), 268-274.

VII. "THE TWO GENTLEMEN OF VERONA."

Danby, John F. "Shakespeare Criticism and *Two Gentlemen of Verona*," *Critical Quarterly*, II (1960), 309-321.

Atkinson, Dorothy F. "The Source of *The Two Gentlemen of Verona*," *Studies in Philology*, XL (1944), 223-234.

Campbell, O.J. *"The Two Gentlemen of Verona* and Italian Comedy," *Studies in Shakespeare, Milton, and Donne*. Ann Arbor: University of Michigan Press, 1925, 49-63.

Sargent, Ralph. "Sir Thomas Elyot and the Integrity of *The Two Gentlemen of Verona*," *PMLA* LXV (1950), 1166-1180.

Thompson, Karl F. "Shakespeare's Romantic Comedies," *PMLA*, LXVII (1952), 1079-1093. [Includes *Love's Labour's Lost*.]

VIII. "THE WINTER'S TALE."

Bonjour, Adrien. "The Final Scene of *The Winter's Tale*," *Englische Studien*, XXXIII (1952), 193-208.

Bethell, S.L. *The Winter's Tale: a Study*. New York: Staples, 1947.

Coghill, Nevill. "Six Parts of Stagecraft in *The Winter's Tale*," *Shakespeare Survey* 11 (1958), 31-41.

Hoeniger, F. David. "The Meaning of *The Winter's Tale*," *University of Toronto Quarterly*, XX (1950), 11-26.

Honigman, E.A.J. "Secondary Sources of *The Winter's Tale*," *Philological Quarterly*, XXXIV (1955), 27-38.

Kermode, Frank. *William Shakespeare: The Final Plays*. London: Longmans Green for the British Council, 1963.

Knight, G. Wilson. *The Crown of Life: Essays in the Interpretation of Shakespeare's Final Plays*. London: Methuen, 1943.

Lancaster, H. Carrington. "Hermione's Statue," *Studies in Philology*, XXXIX (1932), 233-238.

Siegel, Paul N. "Leontes, a Jealous Tyrant," *Review of English Studies*, New Series I (1950), 302-307.

Tillyard, E.M.W. *Shakespeare's Last Plays*. London: Chatto and Windus, 1951.

Traversi, Derek A. *Shakespeare: The Last Phase*. New York: Harcourt, Brace and World, 1955.

Trienens, Roger J. "The Inception of Leontes' Jealousy in *The Winter's Tale*," *Shakespeare Quarterly*, IV (1953), 321-326.

NOTES

NOTES

MONARCH®
NOTES AND STUDY GUIDES

ARE AVAILABLE AT RETAIL STORES EVERYWHERE

In the event your local bookseller
cannot provide you with other
Monarch titles you want—

ORDER ON THE FORM BELOW:

Complete order form appears
on inside front & back covers for
your convenience.

Simply send retail price, local
sales tax, if any, plus 25¢ to
cover mailing & handling.

IBM #	AUTHOR & TITLE (exactly as shown on title listing)	PRICE
	PLUS ADD'L FOR POSTAGE	25¢
	GRAND TOTAL	

MONARCH® **PRESS,** a division of Simon & Schuster, Inc.
Mail Service Department, 1 West 39th Street, New York, N.Y. 10018

I enclose .... dollars to cover retail price, local sales tax,
plus mailing and handling.

Name _____
(Please print)
Address _____

City _____ State _____ Zip _____
Please send check or money order. We cannot be responsible for cash.